PUFFIN BOO[illegible]

Editor: K[illegible]

THE [illegible]

'WAIT!' bar[illegible] dark doorway [illegible] with something roug[illegible] per and thrust it at Sioned. '[illegible] e,' she challenged, but Sioned dre[illegible] Somehow or other she knew the bund[illegible] tiful, luminously shining carved ivory puzzle [illegible] that old Eva had shown her the other day. *Don't* [illegible] *n,* old Eva had said, *it's priceless. D'you sense its power?*

Reluctantly, Sioned took the parcel. She'd not look at it, she thought. She'd not risk touching any of its hundreds of intricately carved pieces, just keep it safe and then pretend to old Dinah that she'd done the puzzle . . . But it was no good, the puzzle wouldn't let itself be forgotten. It insisted somehow on being unwrapped and forcing an appalling discovery on her – one tiny white piece shaped like an anvil was missing, and it must be her fault!

Priceless, don't touch, she heard old Eva's words all over again, but where, oh where, had she lost it? On the mountain, walking with her friend, Anna? In the house? In the village? She had no idea. Thoughts of the puzzle haunted her dreams and intruded on her friendships, as if it were willing her to find the missing piece . . . and maybe to set old Eva and Dinah at rest from some mysterious worry that had dogged them ever since their long-ago childhood in the legendary Drowned House, and the loss of their cousin Lizzie Meredith.

This is a fascinating and romantic story, soaked in the spirit of a 'quiet' Welsh village, where feelings may yet run very deeply beneath the surface and strange things happen.

For readers of eleven and over.

SYLVIA FAIR

The Ivory Anvil

PUFFIN BOOKS
in association with Victor Gollancz

Puffin Books, Penguin Books Ltd, Harmondsworth, Middlesex, England
Penguin Books, 625 Madison Avenue, New York, New York 10022, U.S.A.
Penguin Books Australia Ltd, Ringwood, Victoria, Australia
Penguin Books Canada Ltd, 2801 John Street, Markham, Ontario, Canada L3R 1B4
Penguin Books (N.Z.) Ltd, 182–190 Wairau Road, Auckland 10, New Zealand

—

First published by Victor Gollancz 1974
Published in Puffin Books 1977

—

Made and printed in Great Britain
by C. Nicholls & Company Ltd
Set in Linotype Juliana

Chapter 1

THE crash of china on stone tiles burst into Sioned's thoughts.

'Mum's dropped something again,' she sighed as she paused at the front door, hand on knob and ready to dash out, but waiting.

'That you, Sioned?' Her mother appeared in the darkness at the other end of the long passage. 'Be a dear and go to Dinah China's for me.' She fumbled in her purse. 'A basin it is this time.'

Sioned slipped the coin into her pocket. The Town Clock chimed ten. She was meeting Anna at ten. That nuisance of a basin.

Outside the pavement was sunny and shopkeepers were already hooking down their sunblinds. She stopped beneath the clock and looked up and down the streets. Anna was nowhere to be seen.

Dinah China, Dinah China, Time you went to Carolina.

Wednesday. Market Day. Sheep and farmers and fat ladies with baskets filled the pavements. She wove herself a path between them nodding good mornings to Mrs Pugh, Mrs Price, Old Davy and Fur-coat Myfanwy.

Down one step, up two steps, carefully avoiding the crack on the pavement like an old wizard's nose where two huddled boys poked fingers down a drainpipe chink.

'That was my best marble, boy,' grunted one, blinking back tears.

A flock of bewildered, bleating sheep spilt like porridge from a cattle truck and spread over the road halting shiny cars and bakers' vans. Staffs cut from hedges poked the fleece and tapped the tarmac and bike-boys with sharp shouts scraped their pedals on the kerb. Excited sheepdogs yapped at the black cloven hooves.

An American voice rose above the hubbub and all heads turned.

'Say! It's a herd of sheep. That noise sure sounds kinda phoney!'

'An American,' nodded Mrs Pugh wisely to Mrs Price who passed it on. An American in Nantyglyn! They stared in admiration and disbelief.

Farmers, shoulder-deep in mackintosh, clustered round lamp posts leaning on tall sticks. Farmers who knew her father, her mother, her uncles and aunts and grandparents. But they don't know me, thought Sioned, heeling her way across the cobblestones to avoid unlucky cracks. I'm growing too fast for once-a-week fairs-and-marts farmers.

Hopscotch on the paving stones and hob-nailed boot-print in wet cement. An axe fell on the counter at the butcher's shop with its nose-wrinkling smell of best Welsh mutton. *Grand Dance in the Hall tonight*, and *Lost, One Red Shoe*. A glove hung lifeless on a butcher's hook.

Sioned trilled her fingers along a tall slatted yard-gate and tip-toed across the zebra-crossing of light and shade. Thin Miss Llewelyn with nothing better to do, motionless behind white crocheted curtains, peered hopefully through the holes. But nothing was happening. Nothing ever happened this end of town.

Down one step, down a cracked curving slope to Dinah China's three slanting steps. One, two, three.

Dinah China's brown door.

Sioned pushed down the handle and the door sprang open with a clang. There was no lamp in the shop and all trace of daylight had been blocked out by curtains, cobwebs, and time. Sioned's eyes widened like a cat's in the dark. China plates and bowls loomed from newspaper-lined shelves. Whole histories of newspapers, yellowed with age.

It was a brown, brown shop, silent except for the fading drone of the doorbell swinging on its spring. Sioned stared into the darkness and the dust. The clapper of the bell rocked to a standstill and with a start she became aware of someone breathing quite close to her. Dinah's face loomed into her vision behind the counter.

'Oh! You made me jump. I didn't see you standing there. Can I have a basin please?'

Like a china plate she's been watching me while I stood staring, thought Sioned angrily. The grey face behind the counter rose and moved closer.

'Which size do your Mam want, Sion?' Dinah's voice was like a tape played at the slowest speed.

'Forgot to ask,' Sioned bit her lip.

'I'll show you what I've got.'

Dinah found a rickety step-ladder. Sioned held her breath as she watched her totter to the top step, hoping she wouldn't fall and delay her even further. Anna would be waiting now. And Anna was a stranger to the town. It just wasn't fair to keep her waiting. Anyway, thought Sioned with a horrified shudder, what on earth should I do if she did fall? Dinah was *ever* so old.

At long last Dinah lined up four basins on the counter.

'Are you still at school, Sioned?'

'Yes.'

'What are you going in for?'

'Art.'

'Ah, yes,' smiled Dinah. 'Your Mam told me you were very artistic.'

Sioned cringed at the word but said nothing. The basin was chosen and paid for.

'Thank you, Miss Meredith,' said Sioned softly, backing to the brown door. But Dinah held up a beckoning finger.

'Wait!'

The sharpness of her voice in the silence startled Sioned and she froze. Dinah disappeared behind a stack of china-laden shelves.

Sioned waited impatiently. Now Anna would have been out of here in five seconds. She would have smiled and nodded and chatted and left with her basin without any fuss or delay. With a silent sigh Sioned settled herself on a creaking high-seated chair.

Presently Dinah emerged, blowing suffocating dust from a crumpled brown paper package. With great care she removed the tangle of string, pausing for frequent bouts of coughing and spluttering.

'Now look here, Sioned,' she said confidentially. 'What do you think of these?'

She laid two small pictures on the counter and pushed aside the brown paper to allow plenty of gazing space. Sioned leaned forward to look more closely.

'Eh? Eh?' jerked Dinah's expectant voice.

Sioned looked at her inquiring face and fumbled for words which didn't come. She swallowed hard.

'Look at those grapes, they're perfect.' Dinah's dragging whisper was like a ratchet next to Sioned's ear. Oh Dinah, I wish I could wind you up faster! The old lady placed her bent forefinger lightly on one of the paintings.

Black grapes. Black like Dinah's eyes, and what on earth am I supposed to say?

'Who painted them?' she risked.

'Our uncle,' said Dinah proudly. 'He was a painter. A proper one!' she added impressively.

'Oh? I didn't know that.' Sioned was genuinely surprised. 'Did he live in Nantyglyn?'

'Part of the time, part of the time,' nodded Dinah with half-closed eyes, recalling ancient memories. 'He used to stay with us when we were children and we were very fond of him, but we didn't see a great deal of him, not a great deal ...' Her head trembled mid-sentence and she sank into the past again. Hurry, Dinah! Please hurry up!

'... because he spent much of his life in China, you see, in China.'

China? Sioned cast her wide eyes round the shop. So Miss Meredith's nick-name, like so many in Nantyglyn, had a double meaning!

Dinah picked up the other painting and gazed at it, enraptured and speechless. Sioned began to feel very restless but dared not move. I must go, I must go, I must go, her heart thumped but she couldn't utter a word for fear of offending the sacred silence.

'Look at that flower, and the Chinese vase.' Dinah's low slow voice held on to her longer. 'Isn't it beautiful? Don't you wish you could paint like that?'

Sioned gulped.

'Yes.'

She felt her face colouring. Anna would have said they were fantastic, tremendous pictures, with such a flourish and so convincingly that old Dinah would be happy immediately and let her go.

'Thank you for letting me see them,' she said. 'Bye, Miss Meredith!'

But Dinah had stiffened and her smile had become as cold as a china ornament. Without moving a muscle Sioned turned her eyes towards the door at the back of the shop. In the darkness she could make out the flashing eyes of Eva, Dinah's even older sister. Black grapes again. Sioned looked back at Dinah. Why was Eva glaring at her sister so fiercely? Was it because of the pictures? It was well known in

Nantyglyn that Eva and Dinah were as incompatible as oil and water and it was rumoured that they sometimes hurled best china!

It's nothing to do with me, Sioned thought angrily, backing to the door for a second time. This time I'm going. If Eva and Dinah don't get on with each other, it's not my fault.

'Thank you, Miss Meredith,' she mumbled, flinging the door wide open so that the sun streamed in. 'Good-bye!'

The street outside was full of sunlight. She winked the brightness away. Now to find Anna. But the mustiness in that brown, brown shop clung to her with clutching fingers. I didn't ask to see those pictures, she defended herself hotly as she ran along the pavement dodging shoppers and gossipers.

She paused outside her father's shop door, deciding whether to go in through the front door, which was quick but uninteresting, or to go in through the shop. A glance through the shop door revealed old Emily Prothero wheezing in a corner waiting for a prescription. Nobody worth seeing. She chose the front door.

'Anna's been looking for you,' her mother's voice called from the kitchen. 'Didn't she find you? I told her where Dinah China's is.'

'She doesn't know her way around yet,' said Sioned, swooping the change round the inside of the basin before putting it down. 'I'll go and see if I can find her.'

She found her surrounded by a gang of boys, teasing her and spinning rings round her on their bikes. She was obviously exhilarated by the attention they were paying her. Sioned stood a little way from the crowd and settled herself on the sill of a baker's shop window. If Anna had known them all her life and could remember what nasty little boys they were a few years ago she wouldn't find them half so attractive.

'Hi!' Anna called suddenly. 'I've been looking for you.' She swung round a lamp post and her hair swished a circle behind her.

'You'll have that post over if you're not careful,' grunted Old Davy with a face as straight as his walking stick.

The girls giggled for a moment and then looked at each other.

'What shall we do?'

'Come up to the farm,' Anna suggested eagerly. 'Meet my family.'

'Yes, I'd like that,' Sioned agreed. 'I'll just go and fetch my bike.'

Sioned's bike was kept most inconveniently in a shed at the back of the shop. She hoisted it up a flight of steps, wound it around the counters and manoeuvred it past Emily Prothero's fat ankles. Her father's assistant, Jessie, threatened to squirt her with the last undrinkable drop out of an empty soda water syphon. Sioned ducked and one of her pedals knocked a plastic potty on the floor with a hollow clatter. She muttered impatiently as she replaced it and reached across her handlebars to open the narrow door.

'You were a long time,' observed Anna, trying to balance on her stationary bike. Sioned sighed.

They free-wheeled down the pitch where the air was filled with the smell of chicken food wafting from the corn stores, dipped down to the bridge with the roar of the river in their ears, by the school, empty for holidays, and beneath the stone-arched railway bridge. Then up the twisting mountain road.

'Have you been to our farm before?' asked Anna, putting all her weight on her pedals.

'Used to come to shearings,' puffed Sioned. 'When the

Lewises were there. Had some fun. Jumping in the huge sacks of greasy sheep's wool. Better than a trampoline.'

They crossed the meadow, enjoying the bumpy mounds of grass and the wobbling plank over the stream, and slid their bikes against a barn wall.

'Those are two of my little brothers. I don't think you've met them before.' Anna pointed to two twin-like boys playing by the duck pond.

'Come and see this, Anna,' one of them called, pink-faced with anticipation.

'That's John,' said Anna. 'And the littl'un is Nibble. We call him Nibble because he looks like a rabbit.'

Nibble pulled an insulting face at Anna, showing two buck teeth.

'See what I mean?' she laughed, shielding herself from Nibble's savage pummelling.

'Watch this, quick!' called John. He poured something into a jam jar which was already filled with white crystals. Foam rose and spluttered inside the jar and overflowed on to the yard. Sioned giggled delightedly.

'Put those things back in the bathroom at once,' scolded Anna. 'I bet Mum doesn't know you've got them.'

'It was good, wasn't it?' John whispered to Sioned. She nodded secretly and he beamed.

It was warm inside the farmhouse and there was an appetising smell of baking bread drifting from the kitchen.

'Mum!' called Anna. 'I've brought my friend home.'

Mrs Lind, floury to the elbows, stepped out of her kitchen.

'Hello, dear, nice to meet you.'

She picked up a toddler who was clawing at her, shy of the stranger.

'What's your name, then?'

'Sioned.'

'Pretty name. D'you spell it like that? "Shon-ed"?'

Sioned shook her head and spelt it out to her. 'Welsh for Janet,' she added as Mrs Lind darted back into the kitchen to rescue a pan of sizzling potatoes.

Anna's older brother, Robert, put his head round the door, calling 'Butcher's here!' and in shuffled Mutton Jones carrying a large basket. He placed a joint of meat dressed in crackly paper on the table.

'Hello, Sioned,' he greeted, taking a pencil stub from his ear and licking it before writing 'Paid with thanks' on a bit oi paper. He turned to Anna. 'How d'you like living up here in the wilds?'

'It's just marvellous,' she enthused. 'Not wild at all, unless of course you count my brothers?' A faint jerk interrupted her sugary smile as Robert gave her a sharp thump between the shoulder-blades which Mutton Jones could not see. 'I can't wait to explore,' she added after giving her brother a sly glare.

Mutton Jones smiled, jogging his head delightedly up and down, and sidled out.

'Fat pig!' Anna hissed at Robert, stamping on his toe and dodging quickly behind Sioned to escape retaliation. Robert walked deafly out.

'Do you know everyone in Nantyglyn?' Anna asked Sioned.

'All twelve hundred souls,' Sioned assured her. 'And all twelve hundred know me.'

They walked out through the cool stone porch.

'Come and see Dad's studio,' invited Anna.

They crossed the farmyard. The big barn doors were open and Sioned could see that strip-lighting had been put in.

'That's where they used to shear the sheep,' she informed Anna, sniffing as they neared the barn doors. 'Smells the same, hay and sheep's wool.'

The barn was now edged with workbenches full of tools.

An anvil stood in the corner near a round forge with concertina-like bellows. Tongs and hammers and chisels were lined up on nails knocked into beams. A sharp crack and a hiss from the far corner startled Sioned.

'Dad's welding,' Anna explained.

'What's he making?'

'Sculpture. That's what he does. He's a sculptor.'

Sioned straightened and drank in the scene before her eyes like a thirsty toddler.

'A sculptor?' she whispered hoarsely. That was the one thing she really, really wanted to be. A sculptor! She had never dared admit it to anyone lest some unknown spell be broken, but she wished it with every chicken wish-bone she snapped.

'What does he use?'

'He's using mild steel now, I think.'

'What's he making?'

'That, on the floor.'

Spread across the barn floor was a whole landscape of metal shapes glinting blackened rainbow colours. Sioned wanted to move closer to look, but Anna wasn't crossing the threshold, so she stood still.

I wish, I wish, I wish.

But she didn't know what she was wishing for. A chance to create beautiful, unusual shapes like Anna's father had done? An opportunity to handle tools like those she could see in the studio? The hammers, chisels and knives? Her heart bumped with vague excitement as she watched enviously and at this moment her dream of one day becoming a sculptress seemed to be one small step nearer.

At the other end of the barn Anna's father stepped back into view. His face was hidden behind green-lensed goggles and he was adjusting the flame which roared from his welding torch.

'Does he ever carve?'

'Sometimes. He used to carve a lot, sometimes wood and sometimes stone. But it's mostly metal that he uses now.'

'What does he do with it when it's finished?'

Anna shrugged her shoulders. 'That one's probably for some office block, or perhaps a school. I don't know. I've forgotten.'

How could she have forgotten something important like that? How could she bear to be content just to stand outside, watching? If my father was a sculptor . . .

'Come on! Let's explore.' Anna's voice floated across the empty farmyard. Sioned hadn't noticed that she had left the big barn doors and was picking her bike from the wall. Sioned crossed the yard.

'Which direction would you like to go?'

Anna pointed over a tump behind the farm to where a trail of tree-tops indicated a river on the other side.

'Haven't been up that valley yet.'

They cycled back across the meadow and turned up the valley road. On each side thick hedges quivered gently in the breeze. Cars whipped closely by, leaving the tall grass rocking like waves in the wake of a speed-boat, and stirring up a dust which prickled their eyes. They stopped for breath at the top of the first steep hill and sat under the shadow of a cool, wide hedge. Anna plucked a grass and twisted it round her fingers.

'What's the name of that funny shaped hill over there?' She pointed to a series of bumps on the mountain opposite them. The grass entwined round her fingers snapped, and she unthreaded it.

'The Queen's Face.'

'The Queen's Face?' repeated Anna disbelievingly. 'Ah, yes!' She drew her finger along the horizon. 'Queen Victoria's profile. Big closed eyelids, nose, chins. Queen Victoria at rest for ever.' She imitated the face of the sleeping stone queen and they both giggled.

'What was it called before Queen Victoria reigned?'

'I expect it had a Welsh name.'

'Why don't you speak Welsh?' Anna turned to her accusingly.

Sioned snatched a handful of hawthorn leaves from the hedge above her, feeling as though she had been pounced on by a cat. *Why* don't I speak Welsh? *Why*? A small angry spark that was always buried deep inside her threatened to explode and she poured silence over it like cold water. I can't even speak my own language, she thought bitterly. It's like being dumb. She glanced sideways at Anna. Anna, lively and cheerful and never lost for words. Anna wouldn't understand. She shrugged her shoulders as though she didn't care about the silly old-fashioned language which was disappearing.

'If I were Welsh like you, I'd speak it,' Anna chattered, hoping to smother Sioned's uncomfortable silence with prattling. 'Lots of Welsh people do. I've heard them in Aberystwyth. It's a funny language though, isn't it? All spluttering and hissing and spitting.'

'It's the oldest living language,' Sioned said calmly although she felt like shouting. Her fingers shook with indignation at such insults thrown at the beloved language she couldn't even claim to understand. It was a good language, but no one in Nantyglyn was looking after it.

'Can't you say anything in Welsh at all?'

Sioned spat out a grass she had been chewing.

'*Mae hen wlad fy nhadau yn anwyl i mi*,' she declared sourly.

Anna gaped elaborately.

'That sounds great,' she cried with a dramatic flourish. 'You can speak Welsh. Say some more. Teach me a bit.'

Sioned shook her head.

'It's only the first line of the National Anthem.'

'What else do you know?'

Aspirate and nasal mutations, conjugations, diphthongs.

'Nothing,' she said. 'Nothing of any use.'

She had bought herself a set of Welsh books, secondhand, and had religiously waded through the exercises and grammar and had learnt miles and miles of vocabulary right up to the beginning of Book Four. But there was no one to speak to in Nantyglyn. The milkman came from South Wales. He spoke Welsh, but he had only snorted derisively when she had greeted him one morning with 'Sut mae'n heddiw?', hopeful of a small conversation. There was no one else.

'Shall we go up there one day?' Anna's voice interrupted her thoughts.

'Where?' Sioned blinked.

'The Queen's Face.'

Sioned looked at the huge rock profile carved along the skyline. It was a long time since she had climbed it. It would be good to take Anna up there, then show her Wales spread around as far as the eye could see. Whatever she thought of the language, she'd be bound to be overwhelmed by the mountains, by being alone and small amongst the huge masses of rocks. Yes, Anna would be able to see what Wales was really like.

'Good idea. We'll spend a day up there and take a picnic.'

'The first fine day after this one?'

'The first fine day,' agreed Sioned. 'Early.'

'And where are we going now?'

'Mm – let's go up Pedlar's Lane. There's a little wood . . .'

They found Pedlar's overgrown Lane, dumped their bikes and threaded their way along and upwards like explorers in a jungle. Brambles clawed their hair and scratched their bare legs, and their feet jerked in hardened ruts beneath the undergrowth. The lane opened out into a thicket of miniature oak trees laced with a labyrinth of twisting pathways, blocked at frequent intervals by anthills. They dropped bits of twig and leaves on to the ants and watched their busy and calculated activity as they removed them.

'I wonder how they do so well without talking?' pondered Anna. 'I'd hate not to be able to talk.'

'Silent, secret signals,' suggested Sioned. 'Better than talking.'

They stopped tormenting the ants and chose a track which stitched its way in unpredictable loops and bends to the far side of the wood. They leaned on a small wooden stile and gazed out over another valley, spread like a map at their feet. Cars sped up the road far to their left looking like toys.

'Where do they all go?' inquired Anna. 'There are dozens of cars, but no sign of human habitation anywhere. They look like ants, all heading in the same direction.'

'They'll be visitors,' said Sioned. 'They'll be going up the valley to look at the dams.'

'Why do they want to look at dams?' puzzled Anna.

'Oh, the lakes are lovely,' Sioned assured her. She sprawled across the top of the stile and stared longingly at the cars funnelling between the narrowing mountains. Going up there was like going to the sea-side. When the sun shone, that was where you yearned to be. Sioned gazed mesmerized by the regularity of the traffic flow as cars appeared and disappeared along the ribbon of road below. A strange urge enveloped her like thirst. A compelling desire to see the lakes. She looked at her watch. It was late. Too late to go now.

'I'll take you there,' she told Anna. 'Before the gorse and heather are over.'

'But we'll go to the Queen's Face first,' insisted Anna. 'On the first fine day.'

Sioned looked back across the wood. It wasn't a Queen's

Face from this angle, wasn't nearly so inviting. It looked cold and bleak. The valley looked warm and enticing.

'You promised.'

'All right,' said Sioned. 'The Queen's Face first. Then the valley.'

'Lend us your bike, Sioned? Just for two days?'

Sioned, one foot on the ground, turned in her saddle. Freckled Sammy Watkins squinted up at her.

'What for?'

'We're 'avin' a fair.'

Sioned looked curiously to where Sammy indicated. On a piece of waste ground some boys were making see-saws, while others were tying bikes to the extended spokes of a cartwheel balanced precariously on an upturned box.

'See? We need another bike. The roundabout dunna work with a' odd number.'

Sioned studied the half-made roundabout.

'Do you have to pedal it yourself?'

'Yep.'

'That's a bit of a swindle, isn't it?'

''Sonly a penny a time, gel.'

Sioned shook her head firmly.

'You can't have my bike.'

'Comin' to the fair, then?'

'Might. What's it in aid of?'

'Us.'

Sioned swung her bike round and pedalled down the street. She'd tell Anna's little brothers about the fair. They would be sure to revel in it even if it did mean pedalling your own roundabout. She sailed past a row of straight Victorian houses and a hoarding full of markets, fairs and flower shows.

'Sss! Sss! Sioned! 'Ere!'

Sioned braked sharply. What did old Eva want, hissing at her through the almost closed side door? Sioned wheeled her bike towards her, a question on her face.

'Put your bike in the back yard. I want you to see something.'

She dumped her bike and squeezed through the door. It snapped shut behind her like a mousetrap.

Inside Eva's house it was just as dark and brown as Dinah's shop. Cobwebs covered the window panes like net curtains and artistically arranged plastic flowers faded near the window. A broken light bulb dangled dangerously from its socket. Eva led her through the scullery into the kitchen, past a grandfather clock which had no hands but ticked the centuries away nevertheless. She bent down awkwardly and pulled out a black trunk from beneath the fringe of a tattered plush table cloth of questionable colour on a wobbly table.

'Chinese things that Uncle brought back,' she grunted as she lifted the heavy lid. It dropped back with a screech and rebounded on its leather hinges.

Sioned gasped. Nestled in the chest were soft cloths in glowing colours and strange things that sparkled in spite of the absence of light. Eva proceeded to pull out robes and jewellery and trinkets and spread them excitedly before her like a feast, across the table, over chairs and upside-down splintered tea-chests, and on the floor. Sioned was thankful that she was planted firmly on both feet for in a trice every square inch was buried beneath oriental glitter. She could do nothing but stare in silent amazement.

A colourless cat, bristly as a scrubbing brush, sniffed inquisitively round the bottom of the door. Eva's eyes lit up like oil and she leapt into life.

'Askit! Askit! You nosy ole cat!' she screeched, slinging an invisible missile at it which Sioned, balanced delicately on her small square foot of ground, hastened to avoid without toppling. Eva would be a fair shot with the best china, she considered. The scrubbing brush cat pondered awhile and then, without so much as a twitch of its whiskers or a wave of its tail, it sauntered away.

Eva lifted the empty top section of the trunk tenderly by its two worn loops and spread even more riches out on the floor. There were garments embroidered with birds and snakes and dragons, and white robes glistening with gold thread.

'See this, Sioned,' whispered Eva, slipping a glossy garment over her buttonless fawn cardigan. She held her head high like a top model posing for photographers and turned elegantly on her newspaper-stuffed slippers.

'It's beautiful,' said Sioned, her voice filled with wonder. She suddenly oozed with affection for these two eccentric old ladies who did not care for such mundane things as sweeping away cobwebs, or dusting, but who kept treasure under their kitchen table. She looked towards the window. From this viewpoint the spiders' webs were far more beautiful than thin Miss Llewelyn's spotless crocheted curtains.

'I didn't know you had such treasures, Miss Meredith.'

Eva leaned uncomfortably close to her ear.

'They are treasures, Sioned fach, every single one of them,' she said. 'We don't often show them to anyone. No one has seen them now for . . .' – she closed her eyes and counted – '. . . about seventy years.'

Why me? Why me? wondered Sioned, uncertain how to take such an honour bestowed on her.

'You're like us, you see, m'dear,' Eva said as though in answer to her thoughts. 'You appreciate beautiful things, don't you? Not just for the money they'd fetch, but because they are beautiful, and because someone has made them.'

Sioned wasn't sure whether she liked being grouped with Eva and Dinah as a similar being, but she nodded understandingly.

'When you see real beautiful things like these,' Eva went on, 'other things don't matter. You can sense the power that beautiful things have? Eh? Eh?'

'Er – yes,' said Sioned hastily. It seemed the only answer.

'Try this on, Sioned,' urged Eva. 'This belonged to a Chinese prince. Look at the length of it! He must have been more than seven feet tall.'

'Oh, no, I couldn't.'

But Eva had already draped her in a robe embroidered from neck to hem in jewelled peacocks.

'Stand on that chair,' she rapped out in a voice which could not be disobeyed.

Standing on the chair in the Chinese robe and towering over Eva, Sioned was aware of the hem just touching the floor lightly.

'See how tall he was?' Eva was almost hopping with pleasure.

Sioned looked down at the exotic birds, and stood erect, as she was sure a Chinese prince seven feet tall would have stood. All around her, embroidered trees clustered in valleys of silk, in a strange kingdom inhabited by snakes and dragons, and pagodas stood majestically on hillsides as a sunbeam cut through the dust, plunging valleys into darkness and making hilltops dazzle. It was a magical glimpse into China, and for a moment she almost believed she was there. Her eyes wandered. Eva was standing silent in the brownness of the room. Cobwebs, pink plastic flowers, peacocks and pagodas became confused. Sioned shook herself out of her imaginings.

'They're wonderful, really they are,' she dared to commit herself.

'There's one thing you must see before you go,' said Eva mysteriously. She delved into the trunk and held up a small intricately carved white cube, and placed it on the table as though at any moment it might explode.

'Don't touch it!' Her sharp voice ran like a needle through Sioned.

What is it? thought Sioned but dared not ask for fear her words would light the blue touch-paper.

'It's a puzzle. Like a jigsaw puzzle. But solid,' Eva told her passionately. She lowered her voice. 'Three hundred and forty-three pieces, all carved in ivory.'

'Seven cubed,' said Sioned, and blinked in surprise at her own voice. How had that conclusion slipped so cleanly into her head without the usual counting and crossing-out and endless trial and error muddling usually associated with cube-rooting?

The ivory cube sat on the table staring back at Sioned's awestruck eyes. Eva was still and silent, too, her gloating eyes darting like a bird's to watch for Sioned's reaction.

But Sioned was speechless. Of all the treasure strewn about the room this one small glowing piece of ivory held her open-mouthed and blank-eyed, compelling her gaze until everything else around it blurred. As though it were suddenly in command of her soul, forcing her eyes to stare, reaching out towards her in an effort to grasp her mind, giving out signals she knew not how to receive. She felt herself shaking slightly. What does it want of me? she thought desperately.

She tried to blink, to look away, but her eyes would not relinquish the bewitching image which lay before them like a golden apple.

At last Eva's voice scratched the silence.

'Power,' she whispered. 'D'you sense its power? Its strange power?'

Sioned glanced at the rapt countenance beside her and felt her neck shiver. She gripped her hands until the nails cut into her palms. Was old Eva all there?

'A dealer came once,' said Eva, suddenly escaping from

her trance. 'He said this puzzle was priceless. Priceless, he said.'

No wonder she had shrieked, 'Don't touch!'

'Do all the pieces fit together in a certain order?' Sioned inquired timidly.

'Yes, yes,' muttered Eva and Sioned nodded. I used to have a pig like that once, a wooden one, made in Japan. Aloud she ventured to say,

'Have you ever done it?'

Eva hesitated, and then grunted. Did that mean yes?

'And was it difficult to take to pieces?'

'Yes. But far more difficult to put back. Don't touch!'

'I – I wouldn't,' promised Sioned.

Eva started to pack the things back into the trunk and Sioned sensed that the entertainment was over as quickly as it had begun.

'Shall I go now, or would you like me to help?'

Eva waved her hand towards the door without looking up.

'Good-bye then! Thank you ever so much.'

Eva looked up for the last time.

'Don't tell 'er!' She pointed her thumb towards Dinah's shop. Sioned shook her head vaguely and left. The side door creaked open and snapped shut again. Sioned pushed her bike down into the lane.

'Seven by seven by seven,' she sorted out the numbers in her head, and said slowly, 'Seven cubed is three hundred and forty three!'

Chapter 2

SIONED was sitting at the kitchen table when her mother came in.

'What's that you're drawing?'

'Dinah China's shop.'

'That's very good,' said Mrs Jones in an admiring tone which slightly irritated Sioned. 'I'll show it to her. She'd be pleased to think that you've chosen to draw her shop.'

Sioned snatched up her sketch book and held it tightly. 'You won't,' she said defiantly. 'And why did you tell Dinah I was "artistic"?'

'Because you are, dear.'

'But you don't have to advertize it,' muttered Sioned disagreeably.

'And you don't have to hide your light under a bushel.'

Still clutching her book Sioned ran upstairs to her bedroom. The real reason she had not wanted her mother to dip into her drawings was because underneath the picture of Dinah's shop there was a portrait of Eva incongruously dressed in Chinese apparel, and another picture of the squalid kitchen bestrewn with treasure. She tore out the secret pages and pushed them into a drawer, leaning on it gently to close it. If Eva had wanted limelight to fall on her treasure she would have donated it to a museum, not hidden it under her kitchen table.

A few days later Sioned took the picture of Dinah's shop

to show Eva and Dinah. She felt that she owed the Meredith sisters something. Perhaps it would cast a little pleasure in their direction even if the drawing wasn't too good. She clanged through the brown door.

'Hello, Sioned!' Dinah's deep voice greeted her as though it had been expecting her. The cogwheels were ticking a little faster this morning. 'I was just thinking of you.'

'Oh?'

But no reply came.

'I've drawn a picture of your shop. It's not very good but I thought you and your sister might like to see it.' Sioned handed her the open book. Dinah beamed.

'Let me take it to the light.'

She hobbled to the shop door almost kicking over piles of china on her way and propped it open with her foot.

'It is good, Sion, very good indeed. I think you'll do well to take up art. All those little handles! And you've got the light and darkness and atmosphere beautifully.'

'That's what I was trying to get,' said Sioned, half expecting Dinah to scribble a comment in the bottom right-hand corner. But how strange, how very strange, that Dinah could appreciate the odd atmosphere held in her own little shop when it was her very presence which helped to create it! Dinah had made no mention of her own portrait standing shadily behind the counter. Perhaps she thought it was a plate.

'Would your sister like to see it?'

'She's out,' declared Dinah abruptly. Sioned reflected that she had never in her life seen either sister *out*.

'Wait!' barked Dinah, and scuffled like a mouse through the dark doorway at the back of the shop. She returned with something in an old piece of torn newspaper and thrust it at Sioned.

Sioned shrank back and drew in a breath of alarm. It

seemed absurd, *but she knew what was in it.* Don't take it, she implored her outstretching hand. But it heeded not and helplessly she let the bundle drop into her waiting palm. She knew exactly what was inside the crumpled paper, obscured and shapeless though it was.

'A little problem for you to solve,' Dinah challenged. 'I think you're the one to do it.'

'Thank you,' said Sioned faintly. 'I – I promise I'll bring it back safely.'

'When you've solved the problem,' Dinah wagged a crooked finger at her.

She left Dinah nodding contentedly behind the counter in rhythm with the bell nodding on its spring.

Don't touch! Eva had said.

Priceless! Eva had said.

Don't tell her! Eva had said!

Sioned slipped quietly through the house door and shut it ever so slowly behind her hoping that her mother in the kitchen would not hear the familiar 'click' which was so impossible to disguise. 'There's daft you are!' she'd surely say. 'Borrowing a priceless antique from old Dinah. Ought to have more sense, a girl of your age.' She mustn't know. No one must know. Sioned sneaked as silently as she could upstairs prepared at any moment to adopt a more casual attitude in case anyone appeared and noticed her sneaking. 'What are you snooping about for?' they'd say. She avoided the creaks, keeping close to the wall on the particularly squeaky steps. 'What's wrong with the middle of the stairs, Sioned Jones? Not good enough for you?' But no one heard. No one came. Up four flights of stairs to the top of the tall house. She closed the bedroom door behind her and sat on the bed. The ivory puzzle was still in her pocket.

'I won't even look at it,' she breathed. 'Now where's the

safest place?' She tapped her knuckles together determinedly as her eyes roved searchingly over the room for hiding places. The wardrobe? The chest of drawers? The old toy basket? The best hiding places were always the simplest. Putting her hand to her pocket she felt the newspaper bundle. The paper was soft like an old toffee bag, too old even to crackle. She drew it out carefully, feeling the shape of the cube beneath the paper.

'I won't even look at it,' she muttered again. 'I'll hide it, and take it back to Dinah in a few days pretending I've done it.'

She pictured herself returning it in mock triumph to old Dinah. How pleased and surprised she'd be! But no. Dinah would know that she hadn't even attempted it. Her black eyes would look straight into her mind and *know*. Perhaps she could say, 'I'm afraid it was too difficult, Miss Meredith.' Her thoughts hesitated again. She couldn't say that unless she first tried to take it to pieces. It must go back intact, she decided uneasily. I'll pretend I've done it and slink out before her black eyes catch me.

She found a polythene bag in a box and pushed the priceless bundle into it carefully.

'Now somehow I must seal it up.'

She sifted through the pencils and old Christmas cards and letters from Canada in her top drawer. The sticky tape she had hoped for was nowhere to be found, but a few coloured rubber bands lay curled up amongst the grit in the corner.

'This will do it,' she said as she twisted one tightly round the top of the polythene. 'Now for a hiding place.'

She stood on a chair to view the top of the wardrobe. She could hide it there, it was well out of sight. But it was very dusty. 'I've just come to dust the top of the wardrobe, dear. Oh, a little parcel? That looks very secret.' No. Not the top of the wardrobe. In a drawer? 'I'm just looking for that postcard you had with the Belgian stamp on it for little Jonty next door. Oh! What's that little parcel?' No. The drawers would not be safe. Under her pillow? 'What's that little lump under your pillow? Good gracious, a little parcel.'

Sioned sat despondently on the edge of the bed and slipped the cube back into her pocket. It's not safe anywhere. There's absolutely nowhere I can put it where it won't be found, she thought crossly. If only I had a little cupboard or drawer I could lock up. 'Locked your little drawer, I see? Got something secret in there?' No. Even that would be of no use.

My pocket, she thought slowly. It will have to stay in my pocket. 'What's that bulging in your pocket, dear?' 'Only a box of sweets for Anna's little brother because it's his birthday.' Yes. Her pocket was the only safe place. The puzzle would go everywhere with her.

She closed the bedroom door softly behind her and crept downstairs leaning heavily on the banisters so that her weightless toes touched the steps as lightly and silently as a feather duster. She stopped on the first landing and leaned her elbows on the narrow window sill. From here she could look out over the rooftops to the hill behind the town. A string of pony trekkers was zig-zagging a path up to the top of the hill, crossing and criss-crossing the mountain stream which had carved a deep groove for itself down to the river. She watched until they disappeared like the Pied Piper's children into the greenness of the mountainside. She let her chin slide down to drop on her folded arms. A swirl of homing pigeons fluttered like ticker-tape in front of the window and curled round preparing to settle in the yard beyond the rooftops.

Far below in the baker's yard white-aproned baker boys were whistling cheerfully as they carried large square baskets of bread to the delivery vans, and slid them in. A sticky bun jogged over on a rack and bounced gently to the ground. A baker boy picked it up, shook it, and blew on it. For a few moments he inspected it, but decided against eating it or putting it back. He finished sliding his tray into the van and hid the bun innocently behind his back. Then, at a chosen moment, it shot out of his hand with the speed of a cricket ball and hit Huw Sixpence on the ear.

'Who threw that?' came a roar which would have done credit to a pantomime giant. Huw Sixpence pointed an accusing finger at each of the baker boys in turn while he pulled out a large white handkerchief from his pocket and tried to remove the glaze from his sugar-coated ear. The boys continued their innocent whistling and hurried to busy themselves in other places where they were not too close to Huw Sixpence. For everyone in Nantyglyn knew that Huw Sixpence, when roused, had a temper like a dragon.

A gust of hot steam poured forth from the bakehouse window and the bakers and their vans disappeared like phantoms in a cloud.

The pantomime over, Sioned stood back from the window, It had misted over where her mouth and nose had been close to the glass. She drew a currant bun with her finger and rubbed it out. Then she breathed all over the largest pane until it was no longer transparent and marked with her finger:

'I must not forget the ivory puzzle.'

She watched it slowly fade as the mist cleared until it was quite invisible and imprinted on her mind as distinctly as a secret message on the mind of a spy.

Sioned bounded down the rest of the stairs six at a time, her left hand diving for the knob at the bottom of each banister. When she reached the kitchen Anna was there eating a hot jam tart.

'Would you like one, Sioned?' Her mother pointed an

oven-glove towards a wire rack of steaming tarts which was balanced lop-sidedly on top of a gas cooker.

'Ouch! Jam's hot!' she hissed through crumbly pastry and scalding jam.

'Well, you should never have stuffed it all in at once like that.'

An electric bell above the kitchen door buzzed sharply and Anna jumped.

'It's only the shop,' Sioned explained, sitting on the arm of a small chair beside Anna as Mrs Jones waited to pass back into the scullery.

Mrs Jones' kitchen was minute. Over the years the shop had bulged and expanded and Mrs Jones' kitchen had gradually shrunk to make room for it, so that with three people in it it was as crowded as the chip shop on a Saturday night.

'Our kitchen,' Mrs Jones often said, 'should be in the Guinness Book of Records. I'd have more scope in a caravan.' And that was probably true. For the table, when not needed had to be folded out of the way, and the chairs collapsed. When they were in use the only passageway through the kitchen was under the table, and Sioned was the only one capable of making such a manoeuvre. However it did possess one, small, comfortable arm-chair which, to Sioned, meant home. Its fat blue striped cushion was hollowed deep as a pie-dish from so much sitting, and the little wooden arms were bright yellow from polish and as easy to slip into one's palms as a good friend's hand. If ever Sioned went away it was this chair she missed most. She hoped Anna was comfortable sitting in it now.

Anna swallowed the last of her jam tart crumbs.

'Shall we go for a picnic?' she suggested.

'Nice day for a picnic,' came Mrs Jones' voice from the scullery. 'Do you good.'

'Where shall we go?'

'I'd like to go up to the Queen's Face.'

'It'll be lovely up there on a clear day like today,' Mrs Jones' voice floated out from behind the oven door as she took out more tarts. 'Might see Snowdon.'

'It's not high enough, Mum. And anyway, it's too hot and hazy for a long view.'

'Oh,' grunted Mrs Jones. 'You'll have a bit of a view, won't you? The Beacons, or the Black Mountains?'

Picnics squeezed tightly into their saddlebags they cycled up the valley road, stopping to rest at the top of the same steep hill as before. Sheep bleated in the heat all round them and the tarmac shimmered with mirrors which vanished and reappeared with each blink of the eyelids.

'Ee, I am glad I've not got a sheepskin coat like those poor things,' said Anna. She looked up at the Queen's Face on the horizon. 'I hope there'll be a nice cool breeze up there.'

'There's just one more hill to ride down before we start climbing. Free-wheeling down that should cool us.'

A passing car blew dust in their faces. They blinked as they followed it with watery eyes down the road and away into the distance. An old man was plodding up the hill towards them, tapping his tall shepherd's stick on the road. He paused a moment and swished it alarmingly from side to side, darting after it as he did so. Across his bowed shoulders was draped a fine white flour bag, and his corduroy trousers were bunched up at the knee with a girdle of baler twine.

'He's saying something,' whispered Anna, ready to recoil from the erratic whims of the flailing stick.

'Yes, but not to us,' Sioned assured her. 'It's only Doubting Thomas.'

Anna wrinkled up her nose, more doubting than the original Thomas.

'Yes,' said Sioned emphatically. 'Really! His mother named all her sons after the Disciples. And he's Doubting Thomas.'

'What's he doing?' Anna slid a sly whisper across to Sioned. The old man was almost on top of them now. She winced in alarm as he whisked the air on his stick as though gathering candy floss.

'I expect he's been to a sheep auction at Nantyglyn. He always buys a flock of sheep and drives them home along the road.'

Anna looked, and could see that Doubting Thomas was indeed driving a silent invisible flock right past them, blind to all else as he muttered earnest instructions to his silent, invisible sheepdog.

'We're the invisible ones,' mused Sioned.

Anna stifled a giggle as her ear sorted out his mutterings.

'How far does he take them?'

'Right to the top of the hill over there, the one with the two peaks. He's still got four miles to go.'

'Does he ever bring them back?'

'Never.'

'Then that hill must be overflowing with invisible sheep.'

They watched him disappear with his flock in the heat haze beyond the overgrown banks.

'My grandmother remembers him at school when he was a little boy. Says he was just the same then.'

They picked up their bikes and rode on down the hill. Near the bottom of the slope they left the road behind and followed the high-hedged lane that climbed steeply upwards. Dried mud grooves and ruts forced them to ditch their bikes.

'It's no use taking them any higher,' decided Sioned. 'We couldn't possibly ride back down these ruts.'

They let their bikes slide to a resting position against the hedge and took out their picnic bags.

'It hasn't rained for weeks. Look how hard this mud is.'

Sioned kicked the lumps of granite-hard earth with her heel.

Ditches that usually gurgled at the side of every road, lane and path were silent and dry, and the river that looped far below them in the valley was narrow enough to step across. They followed the winding lane up and up, and climbed at last over the rotting wooden gate which marked the end of the lane and the beginning of the open mountain.

'Look, bilberries!' shouted Anna.

'Whinberries,' corrected Sioned.

'Bilberries,' Anna insisted.

'O.K.' Sioned gave in. 'You say bilberries and I'll say whinberries.'

They sat amongst the springy heather bushes and quenched their thirst with whinberries until their mouths and teeth and fingers were stained the colour of indigo. High above them and quite close now, the Queen's Face no longer looked like an imposing nose, mouth and chin, but just huge outcrops of steep-sided rock. Sheep jumped from crag to crag in search of tufts of grass.

'You wouldn't expect such awkward-looking animals to be so nimble,' said Anna brushing her hand across the short bristles of grass. 'And they nibble this grass smoother than a mowing machine.'

They followed a sheep-track through the heather and gorse and headed for the highest rock. The air was filled with the scent of heather honey and the bleating of sheep, and rocky surfaces sparkled and glinted in the sun as though sprayed with gold dust. Anna and Sioned found footholds on ledges and clumps of grass to cling to as they pulled themselves higher and higher. Sheep scattered at the sudden appearance of faces over the topmost crag as Anna hoisted herself up for the last time and looked around.

'This isn't the top, you know,' she said disappointedly.

'It never is,' said Sioned pulling herself up behind Anna.

'There's always another higher peak to climb, and then another and another.'

They sank to the ground relieved at least to have reached the top of this rock, and gazed around them.

A warm glow of pride welled up inside Sioned as she looked out over the folds of mountains. She desperately hoped that Anna would share her feelings about seeing Wales all round. Mountains, mountains, massive and mighty, as far as the eye could see, rocking like gigantic waves in an ocean and tucked far below them, Nantyglyn, just a jumble of rooftops as natural as though they had grown there. People would be whistling in the streets and delivering coal and posting letters, but from here it was fast asleep. There was nothing to be heard beyond the breeze in the heather and the continual bleating of sheep. Sioned hugged her knees in ecstacy. My Nantyglyn. All mine. My Wales. Nothing in the whole world could be more beautiful than this spot at this moment but I'm not going to say it. She looked across at Anna, half hoping that she would say it for her. But she didn't. She was chattering about a piece of sheep's wool she had pulled off a jagged rock edge.

'It's greasy,' she said, twisting it between her thumb and finger. 'I wonder how they spin it?'

Sioned leapt to her feet.

'I've got a stone-age spindle whorl at home that I found once. It's just a flat stone with a hole in it. Let's collect some more wool and I'll show you how it works.'

On hands and knees they searched for scraps of wool that had been caught on sharp stones and gorse bushes and bundled them into a bag.

Suddenly a sound reached their ears which was not sheep bleating. They kneeled back and listened. It was singing! Right up here, miles from anywhere. Singing! They stood up quickly and scanned the bare mountains.

'It's coming from over there,' Sioned pointed. And suddenly they saw.

In a hollow near a mountain top across the valley a cluster of small figures had gathered. Their voices wafted on the breeze, magical and holy, like angel voices. Sioned spread out her arms in delight as though willing to fly over and sing with them. They watched and listened, catching only parts of the music as the direction of the breeze varied. Sioned smiled happily, pleased that Anna was with her to share this strange moment, the mountains, the singing, and the sky. Her heart sang in tune with the singers on the mountain and had she been alone her voice would have sung too.

'Why is it,' frowned Anna impatiently, 'that Welsh people always sing such dreary old hymns?'

Something deep inside Sioned dropped like a stone. Bitterly she sank down on to the grass.

'It's "Cwm Rhondda",' she said weakly, as though that might explain. But it meant nothing to Anna. To Anna it was dreary and ridiculous. Sioned scratched the bare grass angrily with a stone. The magic of the mountain had been shattered as irrevocably as a burst bubble. Tears bulged in her eyes and the valley below her wavered. She had hoped with all her heart that Anna would feel as she did about Nantyglyn and the mountains, and felt entirely responsible that her little world had failed to delight Anna. Behind her Anna was happily climbing rocks and jumping off, completely unaware of the turmoil and bitterness that had burst upon Sioned. She was chattering, as always, to the sheep, to Sioned, to the sky. And she had called the singing a dreary old hymn.

Anna slithered down a smooth rock face and thumped to rest beside the silent Sioned. She tried to shower the afternoon with words as though a deluge of talk would swish away the quiet. But Sioned's quietness just seemed to soak up the meaningless words until there were none left. Soon Anna fell silent too, and they sat together listening to the slight breeze and bleating.

Suddenly Sioned shot to her feet, quivering like a plucked harp-string.

'Listen!' She raised a finger. 'Can you hear it?'

Anna listened, tuning in her ears to sounds far and near, to tones high and low. From far beyond the sheep's perpetual bleating she caught a metallic, rhythmic clang, clang, clang. Her ears fastened on to it.

'What is it?' whispered Sioned, her heart pounding.

'It's Dad on his anvil,' exclaimed Anna. 'I'm sure it is. I'd recognize that sound anywhere. Fancy sound travelling all that way!'

Sioned's hand darted uncontrollably to her pocket and clutched the puzzle. The puzzle! She had completely forgotten the puzzle. Her muscles flopped with relief. It was still there. She felt annoyed with herself for forgetting it so soon. She had been so determined to look after it with her life, to keep its safety constantly on her mind.

She was still quivering as though from shock, and the hand which touched the puzzle trembled. The sound of the anvil was very distant and reached her ears with a strength no greater than the tick of a watch. Yet it had had the effect of a crack of thunder, momentarily bringing the puzzle to life! Nothing was more important, the mountains, the sheep the silly singing. Whatever else happened from now on, she must keep the vow printed in the mist on the top landing window. She must *not* forget the puzzle! She grasped it tightly as though to make up for lost time. The hammering in the valley continued. The puzzle, the puzzle, the puzzle, it drummed into her brain.

At last the anvil stopped and slowly she loosened her grip.

'Let's eat.'

They fetched their picnic bags from a groove between rocks where they had stowed them away from marauding sheep, poured out squash into plastic cups, and bit into their sandwiches greedily.

'Bread always tastes better when you're high up,' observed Sioned. 'I wonder why?'

They munched and crunched, as contented as cows, as the hot sun burnt their arms and the fresh breeze cooled them deliciously.

'I've brought my sketch book,' said Sioned when she had nothing left but an empty bag. 'I think I'd like to draw those rocks.' She packed her things away and carefully rubbed her crumby fingers down her sides before fishing out her sketch book and pencil.

'Will you draw me too, if I sit amongst them?' asked Anna. 'Dad draws me sometimes. He says I'm a good model.'

Sioned settled herself on a lop-sided moss-covered stone.

'Fit yourself into one of the hollows, and you'll look like part of the rock formation. Are you comfortable?'

A lark sang high above them and a curlew called from somewhere in the thin waving grass as Sioned and Anna both sat quietly in their places.

I mustn't forget the puzzle, whispered Sioned's pencil as it shaded black shadows in the rocks. I mustn't forget, breathed the wind in the grass. I mustn't forget, repeated the ever-bleating sheep.

They paused to watch a hawk hovering motionless in the blue above them, and gasped as it dropped like a stone, down, down, far below them in the bracken. It rose lifting a small animal in its talons and flapped heavily away.

The rest of the afternoon they spent climbing rocks and eating whinberries before finding the trail back to the mud-track. They pulled their bikes wearily from the tangle of honeysuckle in the hedgerow and bumped down the lane, at frequent intervals being thrown from their saddles as their front wheels caught in the ruts.

'This is worse than a rodeo,' yelled Anna, trying to keep a hold on her bucking bike. 'A prize for the one who stays on longest.'

At last the lane smoothed out and thankfully they free-wheeled down the road back to the farm.

Most of Anna's family were gathered round the inglenook in the living-room when they reached the farm. Anna flopped on to a window seat and removed her shoes.

Sioned hesitated in the doorway. Anna's father looked different without his goggles. He was working quietly and intently in a deep arm-chair, a drawing-board balanced across its leather arms. Sioned would have liked to move round behind him to catch a glimpse of what he was doing, but she hated people to watch her drawing so she looked round the rest of the room to avoid appearing as inquisitive as she felt.

When little Mrs Lewis had lived here, polished copper warming pans had hung on the walls, and brasses of every size had adorned the narrow shelf above the inglenook. Now, with Anna's family here, it was quite different. On every shelf and recess and windowsill stood small pieces of sculpture. A gleaming star shape twinkled on the wall near the door, and a tall curling wooden shape grew in the corner. On the hearth a simple hollowed stone rested beside a tall black and white striped pot. She guessed that Mr Lind had made them all, although Anna had not mentioned that he also made pots. On a bookshelf nearby were pieces of bark, not carved, just collected for their curious shapes and textures, and beside them were sea-shells and pebbles. She wanted to look at everything, touch, ask . . .

Her eyes alighted for a moment on the drawing-board and

hastily darted away. Blue-tinged papers? Architect's plans? Her curiosity was jolted by Anna's voice.

'It was really great on the mountain,' she burst out dramatically. 'Really and truly terrific. And would you believe it? There was singing! Beautiful Welsh singing.'

Sioned stared blankly at Anna, not understanding. Her heart which had sunk for ever on the mountain crept hopefully up. So Anna *had* enjoyed it? Even the singing? Or was there a whisper of sarcasm in her words?

'I'll take you all up there some day,' she declared with a generous sweep of her arm. 'All of you. I'll show you how wonderful it is.'

'There are lots of other mountains too,' said Sioned softly.

'As good as that one?'

'Better.'

Mr Lind had moved slightly and Sioned could now see that he was drawing what looked like a large piece of sculpture carefully on an architect's plan. Yes, that would be it. Anna had said that the huge piece in the studio was for a building. Sioned couldn't pull her eyes away.

'Show Dad your drawings of the rocks, Sioned,' Anna interrupted. 'She sketched the rocks up there and they're ever so good.'

Sioned drew back. Now why did Anna have to say a thing like that?

'I – I haven't brought my sketch book in with me,' she stammered. But she knew, she just knew, that Anna wouldn't let it rest there.

'I'll fetch it from your bike,' she volunteered, running out through the porch.

Sioned shuffled uneasily, feeling conspicuous.

'Sit down, dear,' invited Mrs Lind. 'Did you have a nice picnic?'

'Yes, thank you,' said Sioned softly, clearing her throat.

Anna tripped gaily back into the room, opening Sioned's book at the appropriate page.

'Look at Sioned's drawings. Aren't they good?' she gloated as proudly as though she had produced them herself.

'Not really,' said Sioned, wishing she had never brought the book with her. Anna handed her father the open book and Sioned chewed her lip, hoping that the interruption to his own work wouldn't cause annoyance.

'Very interesting! Very interesting indeed!' he was saying, studying it closely. Sioned smiled appreciatively, but still wishing she had left it at home.

Anna's little brothers stopped playing aeroplanes and looked over their father's shoulder. Mrs Lind got up from her seat too, to view the sketches. Sioned felt her inside curling and looked across to Robert, sitting near the window reading a magazine about electronics, the only one now not gaping at her book. He smiled apologetically across at her and she smiled back, wishing they would all close her book and let her go.

'Have you done any carving?'

Mr Lind's sudden question jolted her.

'Er – no,' she fumbled. 'Not really.'

One of her bedroom drawers at home was crammed full of shapes she had carved from natural bits of woods. There were birds, beasts, and love-spoons, but she had never shown them to anyone.

'You really ought to try,' he went on persistently. 'You seem to have a feeling for solid things.'

'I – I'd like to, very much,' she blurted out.

That's the first time I've ever told anyone that, she thought, horrified that she had done so now. She glanced anxiously at the faces in the room. No one seemed to think it at all strange.

'I'll see if I've got some bits you can have.'

Bits? Bits of what?

'Alabaster!' suggested John eagerly. 'I've done some carving in alabaster, haven't I Dad?' He creaked open the black latched door at the foot of the stairs and clumped up the wooden steps.

'Would you like some wood or stone to carve?' Mr Lind asked her directly.

'Yes, please,' Sioned nodded with shining eyes. 'I'd like that very much.'

John came back downstairs and presented Sioned with a small object. It was creamy white, a smooth, solid little figure.

'It's a chess king,' he explained earnestly. 'I saw some chessmen in a museum once and I came straight home and carved that. It's good, isn't it?'

'Yes,' agreed Sioned, envious of his confidence. 'What did you use to carve it with?'

'Just a penknife,' he said. 'It's quite soft.'

Sioned turned the chess king over in her hands.

'It feels nice,' she said. 'It's rather like an ivory . . .' she stopped mid-sentence and hastened to finish it, '. . . chessman.'

She had forgotten the puzzle again! Her hand slipped down to her pocket and pressed the corners of the cube. Yes. It was still there. But I mustn't forget, I mustn't forget.

She hadn't noticed that Anna's father had left the room but now he came back holding in his big fist a block of white stone.

'You can have that to go on with,' he said, handing it to her. 'It's not very big, but it will be a start, and I can let you have some better pieces later. I'd like to see what you make.'

Sioned eagerly grasped the white stone, feeling its shape, its weight and its smoothness.

'Is this alabaster too?'

'Yes.'

'I've never seen any before.'

In fact she had always imagined that it was ointment although she had never seen any in her father's ointment cupboard. 'Unguentum Alabastrum'? No. But wasn't someone in the Bible anointed with alabaster?

Mr Lind's chair squeaked as he dropped back into it and settled the drawing-board in front of him again. Sioned felt it was time for her to leave.

'Thank you very much.'

She rose to go. In one of the boxes in her bedroom was a penknife with a very small blade which would be just right for cutting into the alabaster. She couldn't wait to start carving.

'Cheerio!' called Anna. 'See you tomorrow, perhaps?'

Sioned nodded absently, her absorbed mind working out what shapes she could carve with the stone in her hand. She passed Robert in the doorway. He was carrying a soldering iron and what looked like the intestines of a transistor radio.

'Sorry about that,' he said kindly. 'That lot all looking at your drawings.' He pointed with the soldering iron. 'It wasn't very nice for you.'

'It's all right,' Sioned smiled back. 'It really doesn't matter.'

And suddenly, with the alabaster in her hand, it didn't matter at all.

Chapter 3

THERE were sausages sizzling when she opened the front door. She skipped lightly upstairs to put away her two treasures and began to leap lightly down again but at the first landing she stopped with a jolt.

I must not forget the ivory puzzle.

The writing on the glass glinted against a background of rooftops and chimneys and trees. Steam drifting upwards from the sausage-frying kitchen had breathed mist on the window, and the secret message had become visible again!

Sioned quickly rubbed it off with the soft part of her forearm, hoping no one else had seen it, and leapt down the three remaining flights of steps to the kitchen. The smell of cooking reminded her how ravenously hungry she was.

'Mr Lind's a sculptor, Mum,' she said through a mouthful of sausage. 'He gave me some white stone to carve.'

'Oh? That will be nice for you, dear. You always were clever with your hands,' her mother said. 'D'you want some more bread with that?'

Sioned said no more about carving. 'Clever with your hands.' That was what everyone said. Implying, of course, that I'm a great big goof with everything else?

She pictured the lump of white alabaster up in her bedroom waiting to be carved. She had always wanted to carve giant statues like those she had read about in *Kon-Tiki*. Long Ears. Her mind carved satisfying grooves down the stone, flaking away grains of white sand as it cut. It rounded the rough edges and gouged away pieces to form cheeks which would leave the nose raised slightly. She twirled her knife into her sausage absent-mindedly, making small deep pits for eyes.

'Poor old sausage!' her mother's voice shrilled into her dreams. 'What's it done to you?'

Sioned was jolted back into the kitchen. Her mother was waiting to clear away. She jabbed the holey sausage with her fork and rammed it into her mouth.

'As scatterbrain as Doubting Thomas, you are!' With a shrug of patient shoulders her mother began to collect up the cutlery, muttering, 'Always woolgathering, that girl!'

Sioned objected to being paired off with old Doubting Thomas, but then began to wonder if he really saw his sheep as clearly as she had seen the alabaster on her plate. Did he see them stumbling, bleating, catching their fleeces on the brambles, their tails bouncing behind them? Perhaps he did. If it was just a pretending game he would surely stop when his attention was diverted. But he never stopped. He drove his sheep on and on as conscientiously as though each one carried a fleece of gold on its back. And who could deny that it did? What was the difference between Doubting Thomas driving invisible sheep from market, and Sioned Jones carving a sausage that had changed in her mind to alabaster? A hair's breadth of difference, she decided, and resolved to improve herself, and go carefully.

She pushed all ideas of carving to the back of her mind, stacked up the plates with precise care and carried them into the kitchen.

'Good night alive!' her mother blinked in amazement. 'You've recovered?' She looked suspiciously at her daughter showing the crockery such unaccustomed respect and stood back to allow her to lower them into the hot foamy bowl of water.

'Shall I wash up for you?'

'You want to go careful,' her mother said. 'Your feet are on the ground. They're not used to it, mind.'

But as Sioned swirled the water round and wiped the sausage grease off the dishes her mind rose four flights to her bedroom where the alabaster waited so patiently.

The puzzle too. I must *not* forget the puzzle. Write a hundred lines. I must *not* forget the puzzle.

Throwing away care in favour of more important things she hastily finished with the dishes and darted eagerly upstairs to find the penknife so that she could start on the Long Ears. The alabaster was a trifle small for such a project, she reflected, but she had always wanted to carve a Long Ears, without having to wait a lifetime for the right-sized stone to appear. As she bounced upstairs two at a time she saw herself on a ladder chiselling a huge piece of rock as high as the house. Yes. The alabaster was very small for such gigantic ideas. It sat beside the polythene-wrapped ivory as she contemplated its shape. It was not the right shape for a Long Ears. Too square. She would need a brick shape. Perhaps it would be better to cut it up and make chessmen. A King and a Queen. Possibly a Knight as well. A huge piece of rock wouldn't be required for chessmen. She turned the alabaster over lovingly in her hands, picturing three small figures, grandly carved, standing nobly on her dressing-table where the ivory now stood. Solid little figures which acquired more dignity and character each second as her mind moulded the shapes, chipping off a corner here, scratching a notch there. Sioned straightened herself on the stool, folded her hands majestically in front of her and raised her head proudly. A Chess Queen stared back at her from the mirror. Yes, three figures, King, Queen and Knight, white like ivory.

Her eyes wandered from the three carved chessmen in her

mind and focused on the polythene bag. Ivory. Was it like alabaster she wondered? It would be harder, whiter.

Nudged by a sudden urge to see them side by side she slid the rubber band off the neck of the polythene bag and carefully pulled out the paper bundle and unwrapped it. Hardly daring to touch it for fear of damaging it she placed it gently on the polished surface. It glowed on her dressing-table just as it had done in the dark china shop, giving off a strange, delicate radiance.

It was beautiful. Over three hundred intricate shapes, as fragile as gossamer, dove-tailed and interlocked to form the whole cube. What tools could have traced such lines, spun such threads? What mathematician could have conceived such a puzzle? What craftsman could have had such skill? She pictured a tiny Chinaman polishing the surfaces of the cube, then marking it into sections, and with a saw the size of a crewel needle cutting right into the ivory.

Her hands gripped each other in her lap, each forbidding the other to touch, to feel, to trace the delicate threads with a forefinger, to take it to pieces and discover what it was like inside.

I mustn't touch it, she repeated over and over in her mind, I mustn't. She shivered at the soul-wrenching thought of returning the treasure to poor old Dinah broken, or chipped, or scratched. Eva's screeching voice echoed from a dark room at the back of her mind, 'Don't touch!'

So she stared at it instead, as though its magical power would give her a new inner vision which would enable her to see right into it. She remembered seeing it for the first time, in that darkened room, on that dull plush tablecloth. Even there it had seemed to possess some magical quality. Now, reflecting itself on the shiny surface, it looked quite brilliant. What had old Eva meant by saying you could sense its power? She shut her eyes very tightly. It was still there, glowing with every detail of the fine tracery beyond her closed eyelids.

'I knew it was you,' she whispered to it. 'Even though you were wrapped in a tatty bit of paper. I knew.' Like a water diviner detecting water, she thought. Not seeing, not hearing, not smelling, but knowing, sensing. She suddenly remembered the number that had flashed into her mind. Seven cubed.

Gingerly she picked up the ivory cube to see if it really was seven by seven by seven. It might be eight by six by something else or more irregular still. To her surprise it didn't rattle, or drop to pieces, or snap. It felt quite firm. She ran a finger along its top edge. One, two, three, four, five, six, seven. She ran a finger down its side. Seven again. It seemed likely now that every edge would have seven pieces, and each side forty-nine. She turned it over to glance at the other edge, and almost yelped in horror.

There was a *hole* in it!

Her face was a gargoyle of stone, and all her muscles felt as stiff and cold as ivory. A hole in it. A piece was missing. Not broken, or chipped or scratched. *Missing*.

It seemed like hours before she could shake herself to begin searching for it. It would be in the polythene bag or amongst the torn paper. It had to be!

But it wasn't.

Perhaps it had shaken loose and had dropped soundlessly on to the carpet, she hoped frantically. She searched in all the most likely places, the paper, the polythene, her pocket, her shoes, the floor, and searched again. Then she started hunting in the most unlikely places, on top of the wardrobe where she had decided not to put it, under her pillow, under the bed, in the drawers. It was nowhere.

As she searched hopelessly a new realization poured coldly over her. It must have jogged out of place while she was climbing rocks, and jostled its way out of her pocket, on to the ground. The mountain! The huge, rocky, heather-filled sheep-speckled mountain. And on it, one small piece of ivory.

She sank on to her bed in despair.

Why, oh why, hadn't she said, 'No thank you, Miss Meredith. It's too precious, I might lose it'? It would have been so easy. Why hadn't she hidden it on top of the wardrobe? Why hadn't she taken the trouble to find the sticky tape to seal up the bag properly?

Why, why, why, did I have to do a stupid thing like taking it up on the Queen's Face?

Her forlorn chin dropped heavily into her cupped hands.

'I'll have to find it for Dinah even if it takes me the rest of my life. I hope it doesn't, though,' she added, seeing the block of alabaster. But she no longer felt any desire to carve, neither Long Ears nor Chess King. There was only one thing that mattered now. To find the piece and restore it to its rightful place.

In bed that night she concentrated hard, trying to remember every inch of that walk on the mountain, every rock they had climbed up and jumped off, every clump of heather. It would be far worse than looking in a haystack for a needle, she knew, but she would have to do it. The Town Clock struck one, two. She dissolved into sleep with the hazy image in her mind of two old ladies hurling best china at one another.

She woke with the sun dazzling through the net curtains and her mind bursting with a vivid dream of Dinah and Eva. So vivid was it that it blotted out all other memories, making everything that happened yesterday unreal and ephemeral, like bubbles. Doubting Thomas, the sheep, the singing, they were just hazy, foggy dreams, whereas the dream about Eva and Dinah was as real as the fingers on her hand.

It wasn't at all surprising that she had dreamed about Eva and Dinah. She had drifted uneasily to sleep worrying about them so it was no strange wonder that they had come back and slipped uninvited into her dreams. They had suddenly appeared in a small room where she was sitting, standing? No, she had been hovering somewhere above it and they had not seen her. It had been like watching someone else's dream. They had jumped in through a doorway like Cinderella's fairy godmother in duplicate, and after tapping their sticks on the floor three times they had begun to dance. Tap, tap, tap.

Old Doubting Thomas had tapped and swished his stick all the way up the valley road. Now that seemed like a dream.

Dinah and Eva had danced expertly like mechanical puppets, side by side, one, two, three, *up*, one, two, three, *up*. The rhythm was still there like a tune that lingers long after the singing has stopped. And somewhere a voice had laughed at them from a table near the window; bullying, sneering, echoing laughter. Sioned sat up sharply in bed, now properly awake. They shouldn't have laughed! They shouldn't have!

It seemed of the utmost importance that she should remember the dream, although it was just as nonsensical as any dream she had ever had. Already the vividness was draining away, fading. She reached out of bed for her sketch book and began to draw, searching every corner of her memory for details. The odd thing about the room, she thought to herself as she drew, was its shape. It was triangular. She tried to think of all the houses she knew which had odd-shaped rooms. Old Mrs Hump-the-Oak had a long room, with a bend halfway down, and there was a curved room at the back of the old saddler's. The Big House up Donkey's Road which had been ostentatiously built like a castle with turrets had an octagonal room, and its lodge had a hexagonal entrance hall. But nowhere was there a triangular room. Nor even a pantry.

She recalled that in her dream the shape of the room had alarmed her unreasonably, as had the mocking laughter from the table near the window. In real life the shape of a room wouldn't matter. It wouldn't be shouting, 'Remember me, remember me!' as this one seemed to be doing now. What twisted things dreams were. She felt glad that real life was less complicated, less full of trifling burdens. But the ivory...

She jumped out of bed feeling angry that the silly dream had almost obliterated the memory of the ivory cube with its missing piece. What a relief it would be if she looked at the puzzle now and by some quaint magic it was there. Perhaps she had dreamed it was lost?

But in her heart she knew it had been no dream. That tiny piece of ivory was lost on the mountain and she *must find it.*

She picked up the ivory cube. The gap was still there. The sunlight picked out the carved shapes in a way that she had not noticed before. She peered into the gap like a dentist investigating tooth decay to see if she could work out what shape it was. The space on the outside surface was square, then it tapered inwards, making a kind of waist. She turned the cube over so that the sun shone into the dark cavity. Beyond the 'waist' it widened again into a long shape. In her mind she formed the shape of the missing piece and searched hastily for her pencil again. She drew the shape as it might look from many different angles.

'Why, it's just like the anvil in Mr Lind's studio,' she declared. 'An ivory anvil!'

She recalled with astonishment how the sound of the anvil clanging far below them in the valley yesterday had instantly reminded her of the ivory puzzle in her pocket. How strange. Perhaps it knew?

'I am thinking of some stupid things,' she scolded herself, and hurried down for breakfast. 'But at least, now, I know what I am looking for.'

'Will you help in the shop for a bit, Sioned?' her father asked after breakfast. 'I don't think we'll be very busy but Jessie's gone to the surgery and I'll need some help.'

Sioned felt dismayed.

'Yes, Dad,' she said resignedly. She couldn't say, 'I've lost a piece of priceless ivory on the Queen's Face and I've got to find it because it belongs to Dinah China and she never told Eva she'd given it to me.' Again she saw in her mind Eva throwing things at Dinah, plates, dishes, Chinese porcelain!

I must find it for her.

She and Dinah were the only people in the whole wide world who knew she had it. Perhaps old Dinah would die suddenly, she thought hopefully. And Eva, too, for good measure. They were both about ninety-eight and couldn't last for ever. But old Jonesy-round-the-corner had hung on to life until he was a hundred and four and Dinah looked determined to do the same. She couldn't keep the puzzle for six years! 'I haven't quite finished it yet, Miss Meredith. Can I keep it a bit longer?' She couldn't keep renewing it like a library book. No, it must be found.

She went into the shop through the back doorway and peeped through the peephole in the dispensary. The shop was empty. She settled herself on top of her father's collapsible steps and eased out a book from a shelf which was tightly packed with Pharmaceutical Magazines. The magazines shuddered and spread themselves floppily to fill the new space.

It was a thick, well-worn book, black as a Bible, and written on its spine in gold letters was 'Pharmaceutical Formulas'. The edges of the pages were brown and crinkled and fell open at favourite remedies and preparations.

She turned the heavy pages over and found a little verse about corns.

Have you corns upon your toes,
With which you toil and sweat, sir?
Then take a saw and saw off those
On which your toes are set, sir.

She read it aloud to her father who was mixing up a prescription for Mr Harris-back-in-twenty-minutes, and read it through again so that she could memorize it, along with all the other rhymes she knew. For while other children had been learning *Little Miss Muffet* or *Twinkle Twinkle Little Star*, Sioned had, in her earliest years, sat on her father's knee and clapped and jogged to the rhythm of

Winter is a-cumen' in
Ipecachuana,
Take as much of this as will
Stand upon a tanner.

and

Little John is dead and gone
We'll see his face no more,
For what he thought was H_2O
Was H_2SO_4.

Thus she had known the formula for sulphuric acid almost as soon as she could speak.

Her browsing was interrupted by the shop bell, and she rose, carefully leaving the book open at the right page.

It was Gwenny the Chip Shop with her small son whom

she had ambitiously christened Samson. He was squirming under her hefty grip.

'The silly little thing's gone an' got chewin' gum in 'is 'air,' she exploded, giving the helpless Sammy a cruel cuff across the ear. ''As your Dad got somethin' that'll take it off?'

Mr Jones appeared from behind the dispensing counter and surveyed the damage to Samson's hair. A thick clump of spiky red hair was matted together with well-chewed gum.

'How did you come to get it in your hair, boy?' asked Mr Jones kindly.

'Fightin',' confessed Samson, red in the face as well as the hair.

'With chewing gum?'

'Yep!' he grinned sheepishly.

Mr Jones disappeared into the dispensary again, leaving Gwenny snorting like a bull at her son's 'higorance' and shaking her head furiously. He returned with a tuft of cotton wool and a large green-tinted bottle from which he removed the ground glass stopper.

'Keep your head still, Samson, there's a good boy.'

'Keep your 'ead still, little wretch,' repeated Gwenny loudly in his already frightened ear, which made him squirm worse than before. The whiff of vapour rose from the saturated cotton wool and filled the shop as Mr Jones struggled with the gum in Samson's hair.

Chewing gum, thought Sioned. If I had a small piece of chewing gum, white, not bubbly, I could press it into the hole in the ivory puzzle and smooth it off level with the surface and no one would ever know!

Except Dinah. Dinah would know. *Her* black eyes would never mistake chewing gum for ivory. Sioned sighed inwardly, and mentally removed the chewing gum from the puzzle. It came out cleanly, a solid little shape like an anvil.

'I'm afraid that's the best I can do,' said Mr Jones at last. 'You'll have to cut the rest off.'

'Cut 'is 'ead off,' suggested Gwenny gruffly. 'That'd solve a few problems.'

'You won't lose your strength if your mother cuts your hair, like the other Samson?'

Samson grinned mischievously at Mr Jones.

'I might if it was my 'ead,' he muttered under his breath.

'A crew cut, that's what you're 'avin', m'lad,' stormed Gwenny. Then sweetly. 'What do I owe you Mr Jones?'

'Nothing at all.'

'Thank you, then. Sorry to 'ave bothered you.'

Mr Harris-back-in-twenty-minutes called for his prescription, breathing deeply and deliciously after his twenty minutes through the back door of the Horse and Cart. 'Thenk you, Muster Jones. Thenk you, Muss Jones.' He raised his hat high to impress them with his politeness, and his teeth dropped half an inch curbing his gracious smile for a moment as he took a swerving backward step towards the door. There was a moment of confusion as he collided with a pram containing a baby to be weighed, but steam gave way to sail and he stood back to let the pram through.

After an hour of prescriptions to receive and deliver neatly packed in white paper, complaints to listen to, soap, hair spray and elastic stockings, Sioned at last resumed her position on the steps with her book.

The clock in front of her ticked slowly round. Past eleven o'clock now. There would be no time left this morning, the search would have to wait until the afternoon. She remembered the heather, the gorse, the rocks, the sheep.

The sheep!

A new hazard struck her. Supposing a sheep swallowed it! It would be lost for ever then. Absently her bottom jaw began to chew as she thought of the sheep constantly ruminating. How selective were they, she wondered? With eyes like marbles bulging from each side of their heads they couldn't possibly see what they were eating, and there was not a blade of grass on the mountain which they had missed, she was sure. They must eat everything, like goats. Those sheep had been marked 'J.W.' John Williams? Jack Watkins? Joseph Walters? She saw a frantic J.W. dashing down the street and bursting into the shop waving a scrappy piece of paper bearing a recipe for a drench written in farmer's best copperplate. 'Quick, quick, Mr Jones! One of my sheep has swallowed something. It will die!'

That would be the end of it. They would not be likely to call in Forensic Experts to a dead sheep. She pictured a Forensic Expert with the ivory anvil at the end of a long pair of tweezers and a magnifying glass in his eye. 'Good gracious! A priceless piece of ivory.'

The sky was darkening. The sun still shone but everywhere was tinged with an eerie greenness, threatening and heavy and still, as though waiting to explode and shatter the stillness. Mrs Jones put her head round the door which led into the shop from the passage.

'Don't go out, it's going to thunder,' she implored, in a 'Beware the Ides of March' voice.

Sioned gave a deep sigh. The day seemed full of sighs. So the ivory anvil would have to stay on the mountain until tomorrow. Her mother wouldn't even let her cross the street in a thunderstorm, let alone climb a mountain. For Mrs Jones had an uncontrollable terror of thunderstorms. 'Tempting providence to go outside in this,' she would warn everyone at the first rumble of thunder. 'Don't post that letter until the storm's over, now!' It was a fear that Sioned felt she had to respect, even though she didn't share it.

'I don't think there'll be a storm, Mum,' she said unconvincingly, secretly praying for a dramatic change in the weather to clear skies. Usually she enjoyed the drama of a thunderstorm, listening to the ear-splitting cracks and rumbles as thunder rolled round the hills, and watching the rain tippling down like walking-sticks until the drains blocked and Little Man Pugh came out covered in tarpaulin to unblock them unceremoniously with a pitchfork.

But now she felt differently and crossed her fingers to ward off the unwanted rain, hoping, hoping, hoping that the clouds wouldn't spill until she had found it. For there must be millions of dents and ditches it could slide down with rushing water. It might even reach the river before she could reach the mountain.

Jessie burst open the door.

'It's going to pour any minute now,' she said, out of breath from running. 'Sorry I was so long. There was an emergency. Samson the Chip Shop was holding everyone up. Trust him!'

'With chewing gum in his hair?'

'No. A marble up his nose.'

Sioned went up to her room feeling disheartened about the ivory anvil. This morning she had felt so hopeful. She sat down and drew a picture of Anna's farmhouse arrayed with sculpture and pots and bark and shells. But it wasn't very good so she screwed it up and threw it in the waste paper basket and started again. The lack of light outside forced her to put on the bedside lamp to see by. It would be useless to try and find the ivory with thunder threatening, even if her mother hadn't been so terrified. She would have to wait until tomorrow, but it must not rain, she whispered to herself crossing as many fingers as possible.

Outside her window the white clouds thickened and built up to great heights.

'Cumulus-nimbus,' she mused. 'Anvils in the sky. Even the clouds are reminding me.'

She stared at the ivory clouds in the sky as they gathered into huge anvil shapes and dared them to rain on Nantyglyn. Rain threatened all day and thunder rumbled on distant hills, but miraculously, like the birthplace of St David, Nantyglyn stayed dry.

She had not allowed herself to forget the ivory anvil for one moment all that waiting day, as though her concentration were the only link she had with it, a link as fragile as a treacle thread which, once broken, would be broken for ever. By the end of the day her head ached with the worry of it.

Before creeping wearily into her bed she crouched down at her bedroom window tucked beneath the eaves. The sounds were those of a warm summer evening. Windows were open down the street and voices and wirelesses could be heard. Sandalled feet smacked the pavement as clusters of children, wrapped in towels, with dripping hair and sodden swimsuits, wended their way home from the river. 'Good nights' punctuated the patter as friends and neighbours crossed paths, carrying chips, or flowers for the grave, or tomorrow's trip money.

A black streak swooped before her eyes and back again, dipping and diving, followed by another, and another.

Sioned threw up the window and leaned right out.

'Bats,' she said delightedly, as even more dropped and dived from under the roof. 'So it *will* be fine tomorrow.'

Her ears picked up the high-pitched screeching as they dodged the telegraph wires and each other, constantly changing direction but never speed. They swooped blackly below her, dancing along the whole length of the street.

Between the houses at the far end of the street rose the mountains. Somewhere beyond them was the ivory anvil, waiting to be found. If I had a built-in radar system like the bats, she thought, I could find it without even looking. But I haven't, so I shall have to look, she told herself firmly, and wriggled down between the sheets closing her eyes determinedly. But in spite of her tightly shut eyes, sleep didn't come.

After tossing and turning and fidgeting, and failing to fit into her usual hollow in the mattress, she propped her heavy head up on a tired elbow. The street light outside cast its odd colour through her window making the corner of the room as unreal as a theatre. The puzzle was spot-lit on her dressing-table, doubled by its reflection in the polished surface and doubled again by the mirror behind it. Eva's words penetrated her mind, echoing twofold, fourfold, sixfold. 'Do you sense the power it has? Do you sense . . .?'

What had she meant? How could such an inanimate object have power? Sioned's eyes played games with the four white images, fooling themselves into forgetting which of the four objects was the real one so that she could play a guessing game with herself. Her hazy eyes made patterns of the echoing squares, altering their shapes, turning them inside-out.

Just a toy, she scoffed. A toy to amuse my eyes. You have no power. I fuzz my eyes and you swell up, and then with a blink I can toss you aside.

Nevertheless, nagged the puzzle, I dominate the whole room and force you to stare. Try to take your eyes away. I dare you. Why does your heart patter? Why are you afraid to look away?

Fear struck Sioned like the sudden clash of cymbals and she felt herself tremble violently, her eyes mesmerized by the white cube with its entourage of reflections, unable to divert her gaze elsewhere. Then slowly, very slowly, like a pawn being pushed hesitantly across a chessboard, *the puzzle moved.*

It seemed as though the ivory was causing the whole room to vibrate, as though electrified, and she herself was quaking with it, startled, deafened, dazzled.

But the night was silent. She could hear lonely footsteps crossing the street. The room was still. The buzzing, the clashing, and the vibrations were within her. Just fear. No more. She dared not look away from the puzzle. She would hold it with her eyes, force it to be still, to behave as an ivory puzzle with such elegance should behave.

Power, power, power, the shadow of Eva's voice whispered darkly. Do you sense its power?

Sioned shut her eyes tightly and dived beneath the bedclothes, pulling their warm darkness over her head. She forced pictures of Christmas puddings and tea-cards and wellingtons into her mind in an effort to drive out Eva's voice and the image of the glowing ivory cube. She would memorize all the counties in the British Isles, all the countries in Europe.

But the power of the puzzle was too strong, so that at last she gave in and allowed it to take over her weary mind completely. Cautiously she tugged down the blankets which were now stifling her and exposed her eyes once more to the stage set in the corner.

The chief player was still commanding attention in the centre, but it was still now, its reflections dim. It *couldn't* have moved! She felt calm now. The trembling had stopped. Her fear was extinguished.

What, then, was this sensation that the room was filled with buzzing, yet silent; flickering, yet still? Was this how the ivory displayed its power?

The faint vibrations died away to nothingness and one half of Sioned began to ridicule the other. It had not moved. What a stupid thing to have imagined! Her tired eyes must have lost focus as they played with the reflected images and her wild, weird imagination had done the rest. That, together with being alone in the top of a tall, dark house in the middle of the night. For a long time she stared at the puzzle, challenging it to conjure a new trick. But the puzzle was still. Nothing moved.

The clock outside struck, the street lights flicked out and total blackness filled the room. Would it, she wondered, move again, without being watched? Had she imagined it, or had it really moved?

Her mind became hazy as she balanced the two possibilities against each other, the power of the puzzle against her imagination. In her mind the scales tipped gently, this way and that, like a see-saw, but never settling. As she fell asleep the two weights fused together and eventually stopped rocking. Had she stayed awake longer she might have stumbled on the fact that without her young imagination the ivory would have had no power at all.

The moon threw a pale beam of light through a cobwebbed window and glinted on a pair of black eyes.

'You shouldn't 'ave done it,' Eva growled crossly.

The clock ticked irregularly as though it, too, was restless in the darkness.

'Well,' said Dinah slowly and deliberately. 'I done it.'

'Well you never should've.'

'Well I did.'

The clock stopped, but no china was hurled. The pendulum swung back feebly and another tick burst into the silence.

'We'll never see it again. Not any of it.'

'We might.'

'We never will.'

A cat outside snarled and spat. There was a tussle in the overgrown hedge. A breeze stirred the leaves and wisps of clouds slid in front of the moon. For a long time Eva and Dinah were silent.

'It's our only chance, now the weather's fine. Won't 'old dry much longer.'

'Talking rubbish,' said Eva rudely.

'Time will tell.'

'You've been saying that for seventy years or more.'

The pendulum at last hung motionless. It would swing no more tonight. In the distance the Town Clock chimed but its vibrations fell faintly on hearing hardened with age.

'Could be today,' Dinah whispered to herself determinedly. Her brass bedstead creaked, and soon the darkness throbbed with deep snores.

The next day dawned fine. So the bats had been right in their forecast. Sioned jumped out of bed and knelt at the window again. Far below in the street, postmen were setting off in their mail vans or whistling away in different directions on foot or on bikes. Sioned breathed a deep sigh of relief. The roads were dry. Dry and grey and dusty. The stormy clouds had passed over, spilling not one drop of moisture. The sky was bright and promising, and between the houses at the end of the street towered the mountain, green and fresh and hazy. Today I *will* find the ivory piece, resolved Sioned as she brushed her hair.

She became aware of a flimsy dream which was rapidly disintegrating in her mind, and searched her memory for fragments of it. A child, a girl, oddly dressed. But what had she been doing? Grovelling in a corner? Digging? Crying? Sioned wasn't sure. The fragment held in her memory was like one frame snipped from a film. A girl with long black hair, just the back view of her, no more, crouching or kneeling in the corner. She wore vague frilly garments, with black stockings, or perhaps boots with buttons. A girl with alarmingly familiar mannerisms, but unrecognizable nevertheless. But what had she been doing? What was she about to do? In her dream Sioned had known, had understood, had shared her sadness. But in waking there was nothing but this one glimpse. Like the dream of the previous night it seemed important to hold on to it. Why?

She probed into each tiny detail of the picture, anxious not to add frills where there had been none. All other sequences of the dream had now drifted into obscurity, dissolved by her waking mind. But one vital point had clung. The room in which the girl had been kneeling was triangular!

Sioned did not try to draw it. Unlike the vivid dream of last night this one was so hazy and fragmentary that it could not possibly be drawn without destroying the reality of it with new imaginings invented by her freshly awake mind.

'Your breakfast's ready, Sioned,' her mother's voice spiralled its way up the four flights of stairs losing very little of its strength in the ascent. 'Hurry up! I've got to go to Aunt Rose's today.'

Sioned screwed up her eyes tightly and fixed the snippet of the dream securely in her memory as she groped for the banister. On the top landing she opened her eyes and misted the window with her hot, damp breath. Then she wrote,

'Please, ivory anvil, lead me to you.'

She watched it fade and hastily polished the window-pane with her dressing-gown sleeve.

'I'll go and see if Anna's about,' she told her mother at breakfast time, trying to sound casual and ordinary, although her heart was beating fast with anxiety for what the day might, or might not, hold in store. 'Will it be all right if I don't come back for dinner?'

Her mother grunted absently but agreeably as she collected her basket and sunglasses and purse in readiness to leave for

Aunt Rose's. The grunt meant 'Yes', Sioned decided. She knew that her mother would leave plenty of food out for her father to find for his dinner, and it was early closing day so they could forget about her, she hoped. Which meant she could spend the whole uninterrupted day looking for IT, *and* she would find it. Her heart felt buoyant as a balloon with hopefulness.

The kitchen was quiet and clean, dark and orderly, when Mrs Jones had gone. It was filled with an unfamiliar emptiness. As the clock ticked and nodded on the mantlepiece, Sioned collected a handful of biscuits and filled a plastic bottle with water to sustain her on the mountain. She'd be bound to find it if she devoted the whole day to the search. It hadn't rained, and if a sheep had nibbled it up with a tuft of grass it would surely have had the sense to spit it out. She would search every blade of grass and mark out the areas she had covered as thoroughly as police combing wooded areas for murder weapons. If it were done scientifically, like that, it would be found.

As yet she was undecided whether or not to ask Anna to help her; Anna, who had scorned the singing on the hill and who had shown everyone her drawings without asking; Anna, who would never understand what it was like to be Welsh and as Nantyglynian as the Town Clock itself, for better or for worse.

She stepped outside the back door and bent beneath the low doorway of the shed to fetch her bike. Would Anna ridicule her, thinking it didn't matter about an eccentric old lady's bit of treasure and the strained relationship she had with her sister? Or would she help eagerly in the search, realising the importance of it?

At last her bike was out on the street and she sped away towards the mountains. At the fork where the mountain road left the valley road she was still undecided whether to turn upwards, and call on Anna, or to keep straight on towards the Queen's Face and search alone. But her faithful bicycle, like a good horse, decided for her, and headed unfaltering up the mountain road to the farm.

Chapter 4

As she approached the farmyard, Sioned heard voices and the sound of revving motorcycles. Three boys from school were sitting astride motorbikes which were rearing to go, and showing off to Anna who was enjoying their clownish entertainment. Sioned couldn't hear what was being said but it seemed they wanted Robert to repair something for them. She waited, anxious to begin the search and hoping Anna would notice her and come.

'Like a ride across the meadow?' Rick Lewis was asking Anna.

Oh, no! Sioned silently implored. Please don't go, Anna. But Anna was jumping astride the pillion and the motorbike swung round the yard and out of the gate. Sioned sat on an old mounting block. She began to despair of ever getting to the Queen's Face.

'Bet she falls off,' said Robert hopefully, crossing the yard from the house.

'I wouldn't go on a motorbike with that tearaway,' said Sioned. She began to feel angry that Anna should keep her waiting with such an important mission ahead. If only she could get started! The missing ivory was somewhere at the end of an invisible thread, waiting to be wound up like a silver trout on the end of the line. But it seemed that everything was determined to prevent her from starting to wind up the thread. First she had had to help in the shop, then thunder had threatened, and now, as if those hindrances hadn't been enough, Anna had gone off across the meadow on the back of a motorbike. She should have gone to the Queen's Face on her own. Sioned tapped her feet impatiently on the ground.

'It's great living on a farm,' said Robert passing by again. He crossed over to a small outbuilding. 'Look, I've got a shed to myself.'

Sioned followed him to an old shed. It was full of old wireless sets and broken televisions, and tools and wires were strewn everywhere. What peculiar things boys collected, thought Sioned. Does he really think I'm interested in these?

Robert was switching on one of his many radios, none of which looked as if they could possibly work. He fixed one ear to a crackling amplifier and turned knobs.

Suddenly the Welsh News buzzed into the shed. The buzzing died away and the news-reader switched from Welsh to English.

'I like to hear them do that,' said Robert. 'I wish I could understand it. Pity no one speaks Welsh in Nantyglyn any more.'

'My grandparents all spoke Welsh, and they lived in Nantyglyn,' Sioned confided in him. 'I wish they hadn't lost the language. I've tried learning Welsh from books but a language has to be alive, spoken, not just in your head and on paper. You know, children playing hopscotch in Welsh and old ladies talking to their cats. And "Open" and "Closed" on shop doors.'

Robert nodded understandingly. 'Perhaps it will come back,' he tried to cheer her.

'It might,' she agreed, not really convinced.

'Why did it go, d'you suppose?'

Sioned shrugged her shoulders.

'The dams, probably. Everyone changed to speaking English when the dams were built. I suppose they had to.

And the children were so fascinated by speaking a foreign language that before they knew it they had forgotten their own.'

'If enough people care, it will come back,' said Robert optimistically.

'But people don't care,' said Sioned glumly. 'Sometimes I feel I'm the only one in Nantyglyn who does care. And what can I do?'

The motorbike returned in a cloud of dust and skidded to a standstill, nearly tipping Anna off.

'That was great!' she shouted, waving as the motorbike swept out of the yard.

'You'll fall off next time,' Robert warned her, 'with any luck.' He dodged his sister's swooping fist and dived back into his shed.

Anna, elated after her bumpy ride across the meadow, turned to Sioned. 'What's up?' she asked seeing the girl's urgent expression.

'I lost something very important up on the Queen's Face yesterday,' replied Sioned. 'I wondered if you would mind coming with me to find it?' It doesn't matter at all if you can't, or don't want to,' she added hastily, with a vigorous shake of her head. 'I can go on my own.'

But suddenly it did matter. It mattered very much. She wanted Anna's cheerful company on the mountain more than anything.

'What is it that you've lost?'

Robert had joined them again, keen to hear all. Sioned paused and drew in a deep breath. She was committed now. She would have to tell them all about Eva and Dinah and the Chinese clothes and the stupid way she had lost the ivory anvil.

'Do you think you'll ever find it?' asked Robert

doubtfully, at the end of the story. 'How small was it?'

'Very tiny,' Sioned admitted. She took another deep breath and made a momentous decision. 'I'll show you.' Carefully she pulled the puzzle out of her pocket. This time she had strapped it securely with sticky tape, and fastened it with a safety pin to the inside of her pocket as an extra safeguard. 'If I take off the sticky tape, have you some more I can use?'

Robert found some, and with the utmost care she undid the package. I'm sorry, Dinah. I must show it.

She rested the puzzle on a clear space on a workbench. Anna and Robert viewed it excitedly from all angles, fascinated by its whiteness, its delicacy and its size. But Sioned stood back, hesitantly. A shiver crept up her spine as gradually she became aware that the little shed was filled with a kind of buzzing. Her eyes slipped searchingly over the wires and valves and switches, and dropped to the puzzle. It *was* giving off those silent invisible vibrations again, as it had last night. But it *mustn't* move again! Not here. She glanced quickly at Robert and Anna, and held her breath. They mustn't find out about its power. That was for her alone, like a message in code. It mustn't move. Even though one half of her was sceptical, the other half wanted to believe, wanted to understand its uncanny power.

'A puzzle?' asked Anna peering at it from every angle.

'Yes. You take it to pieces and put it together again like a three-dimensional jigsaw puzzle,' explained Sioned.

'I can see what you're worried about,' said Robert. 'The missing piece must be microscopic.'

'A bilberry leaf would hide it completely,' said Anna. 'You'll never find it up there!'

Anna had uttered the very words Sioned had dreaded.

'I can't let Dinah down,' she said softly. 'She's terrified of Eva, and Eva doesn't even know she's given it to me.'

Sioned strapped up the parcel once more, turning it over

again and again to ensure that there were no splits or spaces. She was taking no risks this time.

Anna called out to her mother, 'Just going out for a bit, Mum! Don't know how long we'll be. Might be late.'

It seemed hotter and drier than ever before, and they paused several times on the road to fan themselves and to clout the zooming flies with bracken.

'Look at it,' said Anna staring up at the Queen's Face. 'It's huge, an absolute giant.'

Sioned knew what she must be thinking. Let's not bother. The mountain's too big to go rummaging around on, looking for a bit of old ivory. Let's go somewhere else. Sioned stared up at the sleeping face of Queen Victoria, and her spirits sank. The face looked angry against the glare of the sky. Go away, it was saying, go away! She looked sideways at Anna. Perhaps the angry face was giving her the same message. *Go away.*

Sioned slid her hand sharply up a glossy grass stalk, making the seeds shower in all directions, and stared hard at the great stone face shimmering in the heat. Dinah's black eyes became superimposed on the face of the queen. Black eyes, looking straight into her mind. What shall I do, Dinah?

To her alarm, Dinah's eyes were also flashing *go away, go away*. It was really as though no one wanted her to explore the Queen's Face. At any other time this would have made the mountain even more inviting, but now she did not want such a challenge. She too was shrinking away from the mountain. She didn't want to climb it. Something was repelling her . . .

The rocks towered above her, massive and powerful. The task of searching for something no bigger than a baby's tooth was indeed daunting. *But it wasn't just that.* Something outside her was forbidding her to set foot on the mountain.

'Do you really, truly, think we've any hope at all of finding it?' Anna's voice murmured beside her.

'It's not there,' she heard herself say firmly. Why did I say that? She repeated it, as though to test the sense and origin of the words. 'It's not there.'

Anna looked at her blankly.

'I thought you said it was.'

'I thought it must be. It seemed the obvious place; when we were climbing rocks, and heard the anvil, it all seemed to fit.' Sioned hesitated, deep in thought, and confused. 'But it doesn't fit at all now.'

'Can't you explain to old Dinah? Tell her what's happened? I'll come with you if you're afraid of her.'

'It's not that,' mumbled Sioned. 'I must find it. She would expect me to.'

'The puzzle is bound to have some value, even with a piece missing,' argued Anna. 'Anyway, a thing like that ought to be in a museum, not in a dirty old house. They should have sold their treasure years ago so that they needn't live in such squalor.'

'Dinah and Eva have different values from most people. I must find it for them. They would want me to.'

They winked up at the Queen's Face, sharp and hard against the dazzle of the sky. It looked singularly uninviting, shuddering in the dry heat.

'I suppose you're right,' said Sioned at last. 'I'll have to face up to it and tell Dinah the truth. It would take a lifetime to comb through the heather and whinberries.'

She waited for her spirits to sink even lower at the prospect of letting Dinah down, the victim of hurling plates and cups on her account. But surprisingly she felt as though her two-day burden had been lifted clean away, releasing a new feeling of eagerness which surged afresh within her; as though something important was about to happen if only she knew which way to turn. She stood still, allowing the unfamiliar feeling to strengthen, in the hope that she might understand it and recognize its message.

'I feel as if I've forgotten something,' she said aloud.

'Handkerchief?' Anna offered the suggestion willingly. 'Bike pump? Post a letter?'

'No. Nothing like that.'

Something was prodding her mind in an unfamiliar area. She fished in every small pool of her memory, but nothing emerged which fitted.

'I give up,' she said at last. 'Let's go straight on.'

She gave a last look at the sleeping queen. Old Queen Victoria had something to do with it. She didn't want anyone scratching at her complexion for ivory anvils, however priceless, picking at her nose and scrambling down her chins. She had well and truly sent them away.

'Is this the road to the dams that we were looking down on from the oak wood?' asked Anna.

'Yes,' said Sioned, suddenly confident. 'That's where we'll go. You said you'd come, after the mountain. It's not far to the first dam. Only a few miles. Shall we?'

Anna's face lit up.

'Yes, that's a marvellous idea. It's far too hot to climb. It will be much more pleasant by the water.'

A gush of excitement flooded uncontrollably over Sioned as they headed towards the valley. The valley was calling, beckoning to her, just as the mountain had repelled her. As though it was expecting her, waiting for her, guiding her. Her heart beat fast as she pedalled towards it.

As the road dipped they sped alongside a row of tall trees standing like a barrier between them and the sun. The constant flick, flick, flicker of the sun exploding between the tree trunks blinded and hypnotized them and they rode on a little unsteadily. The trees pressed closer, eventually forming a leafy tunnel which curled right over their heads.

'The darkness of it!' exclaimed Anna drawing to a standstill.

'Like a cave,' murmured Sioned, still conscious of the image of the sun imprinted on her eyes in spite of the darkness.

'And cool,' said Anna. 'So deliciously cool.'

It was indeed cool, and quiet, and still. For a moment Sioned stood motionless in the shadows, putting out antennae, groping for the sensations which had encompassed her so strangely. But there was nothing. Nothing but the crackle of dry grass, the rustling of leaves, and the smell of summer, bracken, heather and whinberry bushes. She felt as though a thread had snapped.

With a new wave of horror she visualized Dinah holding the incomplete puzzle. Why ever did I change my mind and come up this valley? Why, oh, why? Where should I look for it, Dinah? She pushed the pedals dejectedly round.

Suddenly it was there! Something was tugging at her, saying, this way, this way. A tingling glow swept over her. She looked back at Anna, puffing and panting a little way behind her. And whatever it is, she thought with a tiny crumb of pride, it's only affecting me! Something is leading *me*.

Her mind filled with warnings of possible doom. Death or torture by some supernatural power? She rode on, nevertheless, her curiosity far greater than her fears.

A whirl of brightly coloured cyclists showered round the corner towards them almost forcing them into the ditch. They wobbled a little before regaining their balance and pedalled on up the hill as far as they could before jumping off.

'Look,' said Anna in a loud whisper. 'Somebody's in the hedge.'

A booted foot protruded from the long grass. It didn't

move. They stood absolutely still, not knowing whether to run or investigate.

'I think it moved.'

'No it didn't.'

Dead? each thought with alarm.

They were startled out of their skins by a sudden loud coughing. A second booted foot appeared beside the other, and from the depths of the cow-parsley rose a face.

Anna winced with disgust as she edged away to the other side of the road. For the stubbled countenance which was now peering at them was dark grey with grime except for a damp pink circle round its mouth, within licking distance of its tongue.

'Doubting Thomas,' hissed Sioned. 'He only washes on Market Days.'

Doubting Thomas had just stirred from a pleasant oblivious snooze in the warm sun. He sat and whisked a fly away from his snub nose. His sheep were not with him.

'Hello, Mr Rowlands,' said Sioned.

The little man looked up. His brilliant blue eyes shone out from the grime. They narrowed as he looked at Sioned.

'Be you Jones-Top-Shop?'

Sioned nodded and he nodded with her, pleased to have met a friend. He opened his hands and glanced up at the cloudless sky.

'Farmers need a fair amount of rain,' he said. 'Ground all parched up, like paper it be, like paper. The house be up, too, higher than ever I seen it afore. Yes, yes. Right up. Never seen susha thing afore. Never.'

Sioned and Anna made small comments of interest and enthusiasm in reply to this information although they had not understood one word. However it was plain from the expression of wonder in his voice that, for him, it was the event of the century.

He heaved himself up from the shoulder-high grass, choking and spluttering with the effort and continuing to mutter excitedly, 'Higher than ever, it be,' as he gathered together a little bundle of fir cones which had spilt from an old cloth bag. They watched him disappear from sight.

'Who looks after him?' Anna wanted to know.

'No one,' shrugged Sioned. 'He sleeps in barns, on the floor.'

'That's not right. He should have a place to go.'

'He's happy.'

'How do you know?'

Sioned was silent. No one could tell if other people were happy or not.

'He likes his invisible sheep.'

'If he lived in a town he'd be put in an old people's home with someone to look after him.'

Sioned leaned on her bike and looked up at the canopy of branches above her. She wouldn't mind having trees for a roof or straw for a bed, and the freedom to wander wherever she pleased. She wouldn't mind having no one to look after her, either.

'I think he's as happy as he can be.'

'What's that track down there?'

Anna had pulled her bike over to the gateway and was pointing towards the river.

'It's the old railway track they used when the dams were being built.'

'Where does it go?'

'Right up to the top dam.'

'Can we follow it instead of the road?'

Sioned hesitated. Which would be the best way? No prodding fingers were urging her to choose the right road. The meeting with Doubting Thomas had obliterated everything, smothered all sensitivity. She had lost the thread again and felt perplexed. She should have clung on to it tenderly yet relentlessly. Somewhere the end was waiting to be picked up again, waiting to be caught by her probing mind. It must have snapped because she had not concentrated. Perhaps she would never find it again.

She lowered her head, letting it sink on to her arms folded loosely across the top bar of the gate, and shut her eyes. But it was no use. There was nothing.

'Wake up!' said Anna sharply in her ear. 'Which way shall we go? Shall we follow the old railway track?'

'We might as well,' said Sioned vaguely. 'One way's as good as another.'

Like the road, the old railway track headed westwards. They lifted their bikes over the gate which had sagged almost to the ground, jumped over after them and rode down the steep turf to the old line.

'It's as bumpy as corrugated iron where the sleepers used to be,' exclaimed Sioned trying to keep her balance on the jolting bike. They soon discovered that the bumpiness was less if they stood on their pedals as a jockey stands in his stirrups, and along the track they galloped.

It was good to get away from the passing cars, the smell of melting tarmac, and the dust. The grass exuded a greenness as cool and refreshing as a drink of water.

'There'll be no real hills to climb this way,' said Sioned. 'Just a very gradual incline right up the valley. Almost flat all the way.'

'Apart from the bumps of course,' laughed Anna.

Between the twisting road and the curving river the old railway track cut green and straight and narrow up the valley, through deep-sided cuttings in rocks, along high embankments and across bridges, spanning farm lanes, its grassy floor mown along its entire length by the grazing sheep. Where the old railway bridges had been dismantled they were forced to climb down the steep embankments to cross lanes, and up on the other side. The track passed through thick clumps of trees and beside derelict cottages. It gradually rose higher and higher above the gently curling river.

'We'll soon be at the first dam,' Sioned explained. 'That's why we're so far above the river now. We'll have to leave the track now before it peters out completely, and follow the road for a while.'

The road seemed very smooth and they pedalled along with fresh relish even though it was still hazy and dusty with heat. Ahead of them the huge grey wall of the first dam blocked the valley. They pedalled faster, eager to see the water on the other side. They dismounted at the head of the dam and peered over the wall.

'The water's extremely low,' said Sioned with surprise. 'It's much nicer here in winter, you know, when the water's running over the top. When it's stormy you can feel the spray right down on that bridge there.'

Behind them twelve stone steps led down to a tall iron gate buried beneath the stone slabs they were standing on.

'What's down there?' asked Anna. 'The gate's open.'

'I don't know,' replied Sioned. 'I've never seen it unlocked before.'

They crept down, pausing cautiously on each step in case someone came and ordered them off. But no one did. They creaked open the gate and felt their way into the cold darkness. The tunnel turned sharply back on itself and turned again, and they found themselves on a balcony, level with the huge stone wall.

'I know where we are,' said Sioned slowly. 'There are two openings like windows at the back of the dam wall. This must be the tunnel that goes right underneath. Phew! I wonder what it must be like standing here when the water's coming over five feet deep!'

'Does it sometimes?' asked Anna incredulously.

'Oh, yes,' Sioned assured her. 'It would come thundering over this wall and we'd be drenched, if not swept away altogether.'

They walked deeper into the tunnel. It grew blacker with each step and their footsteps echoed in the distance. Every few minutes they hesitated, half hearing other footsteps approaching from out of the darkness, but it was nothing. They eased their way along, touching the rough stones with blind hands.

Suddenly it was there again! Sioned felt a surge of excitement sweep over her. She had found the thread! Somehow it must have caught in her blank vision, and it was pulling, tugging, beckoning. This way. This way. She straightened up and held on to it, trembling with a mixture of excitement and fear. She must not let it go again. If she could keep up this quality of concentration, not too forced, not too haphazard, it wouldn't break again. Mentally she wound up the thread with the utmost care. But where would it take her? Where would it end?

'There's not likely to be a sudden drop or anything?' Anna's whisper brushed against the sides of the tunnel and rebounded.

'Hope not.'

'Are we in the middle yet?'

They stopped, and looked behind. A faint haze of light loomed at each end of the tunnel. They measured with their eyes the two patches of light. The one behind them was still more intense than the light in front.

'Not yet.'

When the two lights were equal in brightness they stopped.

'We're right in the middle now.'

'Hope the dam doesn't burst!'

'Water's too low.'

'Welsh Nationalists might blow it up!'

'Never!' Sioned dismissed all ideas of the doom she had herself forecast back along the road. 'What do you see when you shut your eyes tight?'

They both squeezed their eyes tightly shut. Shimmering sparks of light danced before Sioned's closed eyes and gathered together in a luminous cluster like the haze at the end of the tunnel. Like wisps of fog caught in headlights it altered its form before finally settling to a definite shape. She tightened her screwed-up eyes, glueing her mind to the white shape, and turned as slowly as a weathercock, stopping breathlessly where the vision was strongest, as though poised on a pinnacle.

It was the ivory anvil.

Chapter 5

THE two girls groped their way out of the tunnel, blinking as the dazzling light met them. Anna creaked open the gate and they both stepped out into the warm sunshine. No one was about. No one had seen them enter the forbidden tunnel. They raced up the steps and leaned over the broad stone parapet to gaze along the dam wall.

'We were there,' Anna pointed. 'Right in the middle.'

They read the plaques on the wall which gave all the information concerning the capacity, area, and depth, and then turned to peer across the glinting water.

'I've never in my life seen it as low as this,' said Sioned.

'What was the valley like before?' wondered Anna.

'Like all other valleys, I suppose. No lake.'

'Pity they have to flood lovely valleys.'

'Why?' Sioned looked questioningly at Anna. The lakes added so much charm and character to ordinary, everyday valleys, she couldn't understand Anna's apparent preference for valleys without water. 'The lakes are beautiful when they're full,' she tried to explain. 'You should just see them, reflecting the gorse and heather.'

They stared down at the water, still and smooth as a mirror except when a slight breeze frilled and puckered it and left it gently lapping the dried mud banks now stretching widely round every shore.

As she watched the ripples Sioned could feel her heart still fluttering with excitement and in sympathy with the water. She cradled the secret vision of the anvil in her mind, memorizing its gossamer quality, its intricate shape. But what did it mean? Had she spent so much time worrying about the missing ivory that now it wouldn't leave her alone? I hope I'm not going daft, she thought with concern. Daft like Doubting Thomas. He saw things which weren't there. And the anvil was only in her mind, pure imagination. But there was a strange reality about it which could not be ignored. The vision in the tunnel had not had the same shape as the anvil she had drawn in her book. The proportions were different, the details more precise, and the top sloped in a way she had not anticipated. So where had the idea come from? From nowhere? Like a dream? What did it mean? Was it trying to show her where it was, like . . .

'Aunty Patsy?' she blurted out.

'I beg your pardon?' blinked Anna.

'Nothing.'

Aunty Patsy was an old lady who had once lived next door, and whose lifelong ambition had been to read the future in teacups. At every tea party she would ceremoniously tip the cup into its saucer, mutter a few words, and then gaze enchanted into the cup and predict long journeys, double weddings and disasters. The trouble was that more often than not the opposite happened. Every soul in Nantyglyn had been bored by Aunty Patsy's predictions some time during their lives.

'Aunty Patsy reckons there'll be snow up to our eyeballs this winter,' they'd say, 'so it's sure to be a mild one.' And sure enough, it would be a winter of record-breaking hours of sunshine. They shook their heads and chortled over Aunty Patsy's forecasts which never worked, but she never gave up, in spite of their lack of faith.

But even the most scornful had to acknowledge Aunty Patsy's other quality. She always knew where to find things.

People used to ask her where they might find lost wedding rings or toe-nail clippers loaded with sentimental value, and she would suggest flippantly, 'Down the drainpipe', or 'In your Grandpa's green sock', and, lo and behold, that's just where they'd be found. She stopped doing it after a while. Her own powers frightened her out of her wits. She was only really interested in teacups, if only the Nantyglyn folk had some *faith*.

Sioned wondered if Aunty Patsy had actually seen in her mind a picture of a ring in a drainpipe, or clippers in a sock, or an anvil in the darkness. The words on the misty window came back to her. *Please, ivory anvil, lead me to you.* Perhaps that's what it's trying to do! The thought alarmed her and she shuddered, feeling a sympathy for Aunty Patsy and her fears.

'Shall we be picking up the railway track again soon?' asked Anna, slipping on to the saddle of her bike.

'In about half a mile, I think.'

The road narrowly rounded the bottom of the steep, rocky hillside, releasing a new view for their eyes as it curved. Not far in front of them it swerved sharply to the left, across a long stone bridge which crossed the lake at its waist, and there they found the railway track again. It splintered away from the bridge, keeping close to the lake edge and was smooth enough to ride on until it tunnelled its way into a tightly packed pine wood, whose low spiky branches forced them to stoop low, and twist and wander, so that when they reached the other side of the wood they had lost the track altogether.

'Hope we don't get punctures,' grimaced Anna at the prickles which porcupined from every clump. They could see the road high above them, and decided to keep parallel with it until at last they stumbled on the railway track again. It rose smoothly over the swooping road and above it into another evergreen wood, cool and fragrant, where the valley narrowed and steepened, and the mountains on either side drew closer and closer together, gigantic walls of heather and gorse and dark trees.

'Doesn't this make you feel tiny?' said Anna in a small voice, as though a large one would disturb the rocks and cause the mountains to crumble.

Far below, a small bridge leapt across a gorge. Beneath it the river, now hardly more than a stream, poured into deep cracks and crevices, dark and frightening.

'Shouldn't like to fall down there!' said Anna with awe.

Sioned refrained from listing the people who had done just that and disappeared without trace. There were many eerie stories about that gorge, and the legends grew up like weeds.

The track rose steadily until it met the level of a higher dam where they stopped to rest.

'Why didn't we bring food or water?' gasped Anna, flopping down. 'Water, water, everywhere, and I'm thirsty.'

'I did,' said Sioned, pulling out the plastic bottle and the biscuits from her saddle-bag. They ate and drank greedily, and lay flat on the grassy bank, shutting their eyes to the glaring sun.

'Look! I spy white heather!' Anna sprang up and scrambled upwards towards a high ledge above them, her sliding feet showering the track with shale.

Sioned lay still, bees buzzing soporifically behind her in the heather.

Suddenly she lifted her head and opened her eyes. It was there again. Tugging fingers saying, 'This way, this way.' Something was beckoning her *down* the valley, as if she had gone too far. An urge seized her to go back, back down the valley to discover what it was that wanted her. But Anna . . .

She looked up at the rocks behind her. Anna was slithering down, triumphantly holding a twig of heather and causing a small landslide as she did so.

'Got some!' she shouted as she hurtled to a sitting position beside Sioned. The heather was still in bud and Sioned was sure it would burst into flower as purple as Mutton Jones' nose.

'Shall we go back now?' she ventured to ask.

Anna's face fell.

'Not yet,' she begged. 'You said we could go right to the end of the track. We can't go back now!'

Sioned glanced down the valley. She *must* go back. It was pulling her. How could she explain?

'Come on,' said Anna, shaking her bike to free it of stones. 'Let's go right up to the top dam.'

Sioned looked at Anna and felt like a handkerchief tied to the middle of a tug-of-war rope. Which way? Which way?

'We'll go to the top dam,' she deliberated, 'and come back down the other side of the valley.'

That's right, that's right, approved the lapping water. Down the valley on the other side, that's right.

The water level of the next lake was even lower than the one below. The track followed its edge closely, a winding groove carved into the steep hillside. It crossed three small bridges and passed by a derelict wooden chapel.

'Who was this built for?' asked Anna, peering through cracks in the boarded windows. 'There are no villages, or even houses here.'

'For the men who built the dams,' explained Sioned. 'Men like my great-grandfathers.'

They plodded on, the track too stony from landslides now to ride. It took them through a deep channel cut into high rocks where no sunlight penetrated and the air was strangely cold. They cuckooed to each other and listened to the eerie echoes.

'I wish the train still ran up here,' said Anna. 'It must have been a lovely ride, up here amongst the mountains and lakes.' Sioned smiled to herself. Anna was beginning to feel the way she did about Nantyglyn. The thought pleased her intensely and she danced with her bike out of the dark cutting into sunlight.

Ahead of them stood the wall of the top dam, huge and grey and imposing, although compared with the size of the mountains it seemed no more than a nutshell.

'I'm going to walk across,' announced Anna, trying to find a foothold to hoist herself up on to the wall.

Sioned gasped with horror.

'You can't, you can't possibly,' she begged. 'Nobody ever ...'

But Anna was already lying on top of the wall swinging her legs up behind her.

'I won't fall,' she said airily.

Sioned's heart thumped in terror. Anna really was going to walk right across on the parapet! There was a precipitous drop on the other side, and if a gust of wind came suddenly, as it so often did up here...

She dared not think. How could she distract Anna?

'Come here,' she called urgently. 'Come and look at this tower.'

Anna paused a moment, and Sioned waited, not daring to say more.

Anna looked along the length of the parapet, and then at the tower. Slowly she dropped to the road.

'My great-grandfather,' said Sioned eagerly, 'built this tower. And my other great-grandfather made the fish.'

They looked up with half-closed eyes to the top of the

tower. A beaten copper fish, greened by the weather, swung gently and pointed South-West.

Anna was impressed.

'It's like a monument,' she said, looking up at the weather vane. 'You'll be able to show it to your great-grandchildren.'

'Oh, no I won't,' said Sioned. 'It's all going to be drowned.'

'How can they drown a dam?'

'Build a new one in front of it,' said Sioned simply.

'They won't, will they?' said Anna with concern, as though the water would rush in at any moment.

'They're thinking about it. It will hold more water than all the others put together.'

'But this dam is the best of them all,' she said angrily. 'Can't the people in Nantyglyn sign petitions or something?'

Sioned couldn't understand Anna, wanting everything to stay just as it was. Nantyglyn had not changed for a thousand years, or so it seemed to Sioned. The building of a new dam would mean new routines, new people, opportunities for exciting things to happen. Nantyglyn was very dreary sometimes although she would never admit it aloud. No, the Nantyglynians wouldn't protest, they'd be proud, that of all rivers, theirs had been chosen, and excited at the prospect of new things to come. It meant that Nantyglyn would be full of strangers. Sioned's mother had told her what it had been like when the last dam had been built, with Poles, Italians and Scots everywhere, and new houses springing up to accommodate them. Huge giants of machines had invaded the narrow streets bringing out the whole population to watch their slow progress towards the mountains. And finally it was opened by the Queen herself. Things certainly promised to happen in Nantyglyn if they did decide to build the new dam.

The road down the other side of the valley looped round

the long fingers of lake where small streams ran into it. The two girls jumped on their bikes and swooped eagerly round the hairpin bends.

'Hey!' shrieked Sioned suddenly. 'Just look at the island!'

They both braked sharply and swung towards the fence. In the middle of the lake was an island covered with evergreens. But the water which usually surrounded it had been drained from its shores by the long drought so that dry land now stretched right across to the island from the road.

'I've never seen it dry right across before,' exclaimed Sioned. 'D'you think we could walk across?'

Two small mountain ponies galloped away as they climbed inexpertly over the swaying wire fence and made their way down the slippery turf to the lake. The dry winds had sucked up every droplet of moisture from the bed and a fierce hot sun had cracked it into hexagons and curled up the edges. Their feet crunched dryly on the jagged saucers of mud, crushing it to a fine powder, and like spacemen on a strange planet they stepped down, down on the bleak, bare ground. Below the grass-line sounds were eerie and muffled. They dipped lower and lower on the exposed lake bed. As they neared the lowest dip the mud became soggy as water seeped through from a nearby stream, and they sank to their ankles in spite of picking their way. At last the island was reached.

The trees were tall and thick, and the ground untrodden. Huge cones lay in the shadows on the untouched grass.

'Souvenirs!' shouted Anna. 'We'll take some home to prove we've been here.' She began to gather up armfuls. 'Do you think anyone has been here before us?'

The breeze picked up Anna's voice and wafted it through the still, dark cavities between the trees. Doubting Thomas, they seemed to whisper back. Doubting Thomas.

'Doubting Thomas has been here!' Sioned shouted suddenly. She tossed a cone into the air and caught it. 'D'you remember? He had a bundle of fir cones just like these. But – what was he muttering? Can you remember?'

'Couldn't understand a word,' confessed Anna. 'Thought he was talking Welsh.'

' "The house be up",' Sioned quoted slowly. 'That's what he said, "The house be up. Higher than ever".'

'Still don't understand,' said Anna blankly.

'The Drowned House!' breathed Sioned. '*The Drowned House.*'

The old house which had been drowned beneath the waters of the lake was such a unique feature of Nantyglyn that it was always spoken about in capital letters and with great reverence. Slowly the meaning of the words dawned on Anna and she sprang to life.

'*Is* there one?'

'Yes.'

'Can we go there?'

'Yes.'

'Now?'

'Yes, come on.'

They followed the road down the valley, racing with a new release of energy and forgetting all feeling of hunger, thirst and exhaustion. Sioned was tingling with excitement now, for the sensation of being guided had gripped her again, but in a much stronger way than ever before. Something was pulling her towards it, slowly but very deliberately. She closed her mind to everything else in the world and allowed herself to be drawn along down the valley.

Dinah opened the brown door of her shop two inches and narrowed her eyes. Between the chimney pots, telegraph poles and petrol pumps towered the mountains. Her old face lit up and her nodding head sank deeper between her shoulders. She rubbed her rusty old hands together and gave a grunt which was the nearest to a chuckle her throat had ever emitted.

The sky was high, the hills were hazy and the sun cast sharp black shadows.

''Twill be today, Eva.' Her thin lips formed the words, and even if they had made a sound, no one but the spiders would have heard. ''Twill be today,' she mouthed.

'Beautiful morning, Miss Meredith.' Mrs Pugh trotted briskly along the pavement which sloped upwards in front of the shop door, her heels tapping like coconut shells as she disappeared from view.

Dinah scowled at having her thoughts broken into so rudely, and slammed the door. She shuffled back into the more familiar darkness and sat on her box behind the counter.

''Twill be today,' she dared to say aloud, and drifted to semi-sleep amongst the plates and basins and honeypots.

The feeling which had gripped Sioned was now unmistakable. Like a migrating bird she followed some guiding instinct which was pulling, tugging her down the valley so that she flew as though on wings, ignoring Anna's pleas to wait, not seeing the frightened sheep which scurried over ditches to avoid her whirling pedals. Everything around her blurred into a meaningless haze as she opened her mind to the sensations and allowed herself to drift on and on.

Unfortunately she failed to see a stone, which had become dislodged from its shelf on the high rock, drop and shatter, spreading slivers of slate across her path. Her wheels skidded violently and she sailed into a ditch of sharp damp rushes, her feet tangled with her handlebars.

Anna panted up the road behind her.

'I thought you were going too fast,' she said in a triumphant voice. 'Are you all right? Ugh! Tomato sauce!' she added, seeing Sioned's cut ankle.

'That doesn't matter. Is my bike all right?' Sioned dabbed the cut with a handkerchief, patted her bruises and tested her bike for roadworthiness.

'Come on,' she said urgently. 'We must be getting on.'

Anna stared open-mouthed after her as she sailed away round the next bend.

'Hi! Wait for me!' she shouted, scrambling on and pedalling after Sioned.

But Sioned pressed determinedly on. This time she would not let go. She allowed herself to be guided round the lakes, winding back across the bridge over the gorge and on down the valley. Anna would have liked to stop for a while to lean over the parapet and look down into the depths of the gorge, but Sioned had gone on, speeding down into the lower valley.

'I didn't realize it would be so far,' puffed Anna. 'What's the hurry?'

'It's not very far now,' said Sioned, begrudging the breath wasted in speaking. Suddenly she stopped and stood her bike against the fence.

'This is it,' she said breathlessly. 'The Drowned House is down below. Drop your bike.'

As though in a trance she slowly climbed the fence and slipped herself down the steep forest floor. She stood still on a narrow sheep-track, and then followed it as it led sideways out of the wood. Anna stood beside her as they looked out over the water far below.

'I can't see any house,' said Anna, slithering down to a sitting position. 'Where is it?'

But Sioned seemed not to have heard. She stood very still staring out over the lake, as though reluctant to go any farther. Anna was bewildered. They had hurtled all the way down the valley at top speed – for what? Just to stare out over the water?

'Where is the House?' she repeated.

'It's here,' said Sioned vaguely, moving down to the water. 'It is here somewhere.'

'A house can't be that hard to find!'

Sioned blinked. 'Oh, I didn't mean the house,' she apologized. 'I was just thinking about something else. This is the house.'

Her finger pointed to the parched mud banks between them and the water where squares of wall rose from the lake bed.

'Is that it?' whispered Anna disappointedly. 'No doors, no windows, there's hardly anything!'

'I'm sorry,' said Sioned guiltily. 'I forgot to say. The House was pulled down before the valley was drowned. These are only the garden walls. That's all that's left. This is what we call The Drowned House.' Her voice trailed away to a murmur. She was annoyed with herself for not having explained that before. Of course Anna would have expected to see a complete house that could be explored, with doors to creak open and rooms to wander through. 'I'm sorry,' she said again.

'So there is no house?' asked Anna, dismayed.

'No.'

'Oh.'

One of the most exciting things to see in Nantyglyn, thought Sioned crossly, and she's disappointed. And it's my fault. I thought she'd realize.

'Never mind,' said Anna, suddenly cheerful. 'Let's look round the dried Drowned Gardens instead.'

Once more they stepped on to the hardened mud bed. High stone walls rose up out of the mud, with slate slabs still lying neatly across the tops. They trod their way through an archway into one of the gardens. Hundreds of footprints had flattened the hollows of dried mud, and here and there small clusters of sightseers marvelled at the bare mud gardens, drowned for nearly a century and only exposed in exceptional droughts. Sioned and Anna explored every garden and then climbed on to the top of a high wall.

'I wonder what the house was like?' asked Anna.

'Quite big,' said Sioned. 'My grandmother has some old sepia photographs of it in her attic. You can tell it must have been big by the size of the gardens.'

'Is there anything left of the house at all?'

'I don't think so. But the water level has never been so low as this before, I'm sure. The House would have been below the garden, down beneath the water level. Let's walk round and have a look.'

They stayed on top of the walls and followed them round gardens and alongside old paths until they dropped steeply down towards the water where the house must have stood. The water was clear and calm. Smooth dark ripples fingered the parched mud at the water's edge as though trying to climb the steep slope, but each time falling gently back to bounce in the glittering reflections. The thin dark rim paled as the mud drank away the moisture, and waited for a wind to send the ripples climbing again. Their eyes rested on the hypnotic waves gliding and ruffling below them. Sometimes they saw nothing but hills and trees growing in their up-side-down world, sometimes leaves and froth and minute fragments of debris dancing on the surface, and occasionally, when the reflections darkened, they peered down into the depths and saw the floor of the lake, smooth, shadowy and unmoving.

'Can you see those dark ridges in the mud?' said Anna, drawing lines in the air with her finger. 'Do you think they were once the house walls?'

Sioned's eyes followed the moving finger.

'Why, yes,' she agreed excitedly. 'The edges of rooms.'

Their eyes traced the grooves and ridges on the floor below the water, as their feet edged along the wall. Between reflections and ripples and glinting splashes of the sun the shape of the house spread itself out before them like an archtect's plan, wavering and shimmering through the water.

'Look,' exclaimed Sioned high on the wall. 'This part of the house is right out of the water!'

To her left the faint lines ran like furrows out of the water and on to the dry mud.

'Let's jump down,' said Anna, sitting on the stone slabs in readiness to slide off to the ground below. Together they thumped on to the dry mud.

'That's odd,' said Sioned. 'They've disappeared.'

'Like earthworks in an aerial photograph. You can only see it from above.'

They walked round the garden again to where the wall was low, and climbed up once more. Sioned followed Anna back to look down once more on the house.

'There they are,' said Sioned. 'We didn't imagine them.'

They sat on the high wall surveying the outlines of the mysterious rooms.

'The servants' quarters,' suggested Anna with a sweep of her hand, like a child playing house with chalk marks on the ground. 'And the back stairs must have started from here. Then – yes – the butler's pantry. Morning-room. Drawing-room . . .'

Sioned heard no more. She suddenly felt her spine tingling as her eyes caught the outline of a three-walled room. Three walls! The memory of her two dreams flashed into her mind so vividly that for a moment everything else was blotted out. The triangular room! Here! She stared blankly.

There was the corner where the door would have been, where Eva and Dinah had appeared like Fairy Godmothers, and the shorter side where light from the window had filtered through and a voice had laughed so spitefully. The walls of her dream grew in her memory like ghosts and enveloped the little room. Yes, it was the room of her dreams. Her gaze fixed on one of the corners and a new memory swept over her.

The girl! The long dark hair, black buttoned boots, frilly pinafore. That was the corner where the girl had knelt, where she had cried. The despair experienced by the girl now touched Sioned so sharply that she almost wept. The world seemed to be turning, twisting out of shape, upside-down. Who am I? Where do I belong?

She tried to shake away the haziness with mundane thoughts, trying to create clear, everyday pictures, like Sioned Jones exploring The Drowned House with muddy sandals and scratched ankles. But the dream kept merging with the reality so that she began to doubt which was which.

A new compulsion had been creeping over her which she could no longer ignore. It came hand in hand with a fear that made her heart bump frantically, but the fear did not weaken it. It was something she must do, whatever the consequences. She waited, poised on the high wall above the triangular room, took a deep breath, and prepared to jump across the threshold of her dream. She wriggled forward to the edge of the wall, and dropped.

Chapter 6

'I'M going to walk round the walls again.' Anna shouted down to Sioned. 'To see if I can find anything else.'

Sioned nodded vaguely and stood, silent, where the girl in her dream had stood. It was this exact spot. She began to tremble with a mixture of excitement and dread. She knew this was the spot. She could *feel* it.

Sounds changed. Muffled silence again. Like the island. No, not like the island. For the tiny room was becoming enclosed. Her eyes wandered hesitantly about her. Had she been here before? Had all this happened before?

'Indigestion,' her mother would say. 'Nothing but indigestion. Something you've eaten.' It was a reassuring thought.

But suddenly she became aware of walls. Transparent walls wavering, quivering, as though being seen through new unused eyes; as though struggling for existence in a dream. The walls glimmered and faded like reflections in water. They would not be there for long. 'Perhaps when the sun goes down they'll be gone,' Sioned's thoughts told her. 'I must hurry.'

She dropped to her knees. The walls round her strengthened as she did so, timidly offering protection. She suddenly felt Dinah's strange presence, felt a warmth which the old lady did not often exude. It comforted her even more than the thought of her mother explaining it all away with indigestion.

She clawed at the mud in the corner, and then sat back on her heels to ponder awhile about the dream girl. Had she, too, been searching? Sioned was overcome by a feeling of despair. It swathed her like a black cloak, but it had come from outside herself, as though she were suffering someone else's despair, not her own. The girl in the dream had cried, she was sure, even though she had not seen her face. Tears fell from her own eyes as desperately she wondered what it all meant, the walls, the dreams, the triangular room. In the echoing distance she heard laughter, sneering bullying laughter like the laughter in her first dream. It wasn't Dinah. Dinah was there, somewhere, watching over her like a guardian angel. She would be safe from the bullying laughter as long as Dinah kept watch, for Dinah understood everything.

Helplessly she felt her hands burrowing into the dry mud. There was no sound except the distant swish of water outside and the whisper of her own hands scraping away at the powdered mud. In her heart she already knew what she would find but she dared not let the idea form.

She was unearthing small stones now, and stroked away the dust from them to see their shapes before rejecting them. Mechanically she counted the stones she found, eight, nine, ten, a black button, eleven, twelve . . .

The smooth dry mud powdered finely, making her cough. She scratched feverishly, but as carefully as an archaeologist searching for remains. Her digging fingers began to squelch as water seeped through into the hole she had made. The pit widened, and deepened, as she picked out pebbles and stones and pieces of broken pottery and wiped them with her muddy fingers. Her heart pounded furiously. She was so close now.

She could hear voices, and looked up sharply. The dream walls were fast disappearing. The voices were those of children, running along the wall, drawing nearer. Determinedly she kept digging and feeling.

At last a tiny white stone fell with a splash from the side of the hole into the small muddy pool of water that had formed at the bottom. Frantically she dived her hand down and felt round the basin of mud. Her fingers closed on something hard and sharp. She whisked it in the pool to swill away the mud and stood upright with it resting in the middle of her palm. Her search was over!

'Cor! You're muddy!'

She whirled round and looked up. Two small boys standing blackly like giants on the wall above her were staring down in admiration.

'Did you make that 'ole?'

Sioned turned round and looked at the corner where she had been kneeling. She certainly had made a mess. Hurriedly she pushed the pile of mud back into the hole with her foot and patted it smooth with her soles, as she wiped her stinging damp cheeks.

'I was just looking for something,' she said.

'Did you find it?'

Sioned nodded happily. She took a last look at the triangular room. The black button lay on its floor, like an eye. She didn't usually collect buttons but she picked it up and laid it gently on her palm. When the two boys had gone she went to the water's edge to wash the two tiny objects in the clear water. She shook them dry and rested them once more on her palm. The sun glowed, casting black shadows beneath them. She picked off the black one, and turned the white one over lovingly in her hand, and stared at it, her face flushed with delight. It was the ivory anvil.

Anna was engrossed in a one-sided conversation with a little brown corduroy man who was sitting on a low sunny wall, the self-appointed guide to The Drowned House. He was puffed up with pride and importance as he pointed with his stick along the length of the wall.

'Used to run along that wall on my way to school, I did. when I was a lumper,' he stated with enthusiasm. 'Knew all them as lived here, very well indeed.'

A family with a bulldog drew closer to listen to the old man's sentimental memories, followed by an elderly couple in straw hats. The old man's delight glowed like the sun.

'Fell off this wall many times, yes, indeed, many times.' he reminisced. 'Once I was chased by a bull, a Hereford, biggest I ever did see.' His arms drew a shape which would have filled the valley. 'He was right behind me, but I hid in the doorway there, in the garden wall. Wooden door it was. Gone now. I'm ninety-four, or -five. He went straight past me. Hooves like thunder, indeed he did.' The old man chuckled and rocked on the wall. His audience was lapping up every word, and waited for more, but tantalizingly he said no more, merely lit his pipe and sucked heavily at the stem.

'Sss ! Anna !' hissed Sioned.

Anna held her finger to her lips.

'Not now. Come and listen.'

The old man waited until a group of six people drifted within hearing, then coughed loudly.

'I'm ninety-five, or-six, I remember . . .'

Sioned pulled Anna away.

'Don't believe a word of it,' she whispered to Anna. 'My gran says he's nowhere near ninety, only imagines it for the occasion.'

Anna looked deflated.

'Perhaps you're right,' she admitted. 'He doesn't seem to know how old he is himself.'

She hung back to listen to his fantasies while Sioned sat on a wall out of his sight and waited. Buried inside her clenched hand lay the anvil, precious as a diamond. She gazed at it. Soon it would be back in its place. They would take it back to the farm, open the packet containing the puzzle and click it into its cavity. And tomorrow she would return it triumphantly to Dinah. Her heart danced at the thought. The three terrible days of worry were worth enduring for this one moment. She tilted her palm and the ivory turned. It was exactly the shape she had predicted.

The old man would have gone on for hours but for the arrival of someone from Nantyglyn. He coughed in the middle of a fascinating story, leaving his listeners suspended in mid-air, their ears open. But no more came.

'Canna stay here all day. Got to be off.'

'At it again, John Jenks?'

'Hello, Mary, gel! Beautiful weather we're having. Bit dry though?'

Anna stretched herself and skipped over to Sioned. 'What did you want?' she asked.

Sioned grinned helplessly as she opened her hand.

'Look what I've just found!'

Anna looked at the ivory in her hand, slowly realizing the significance of the grin.

'Is that it?' she blinked. 'You found it? Here?'

Sioned nodded.

'But how? Where?'

Sioned pointed towards the water's edge.

'Down there, in one of those rooms.'

Deep under the mud with gritty pebbles and pottery and shoe-buttons. She opened her other hand. Could it be a shoe-button from one of the black buttoned boots? She quickly closed her hand again. It was too puzzling.

'However did it get there?' Anna persisted. 'You thought you'd lost it on the mountain.'

'I don't know,' said Sioned softly. She didn't want to work it out, didn't want to ask herself questions. She just wanted to rejoice in the finding of it.

'I suppose someone must have found it after you'd dropped it, and lost it again here?' suggested Anna.

Sioned's face shone with a beam of relief.

'Of course,' she said. 'That's what must have happened.'

But there was an uneasy feeling deep inside her which denied that explanation. However, the feeling was a distant one and she pushed it away even further. Anna's explanation would do very well for now.

Looking back at The Drowned House as they climbed up to the road, Sioned could see the walls, the old man, the sightseers, the bulldog. How very ordinary they all looked. No glimmer of ghostly walls. No feeling of intruding into another dimension. Just the ivory anvil in her hand, and the shoe-button. Yes, Anna's explanation would do for now.

'But how did you know where to look for it?' puzzled Anna as they sailed back down the valley to Nantyglyn. 'We might have been all day searching on the mountain.'

'I just had a feeling . . .' began Sioned cautiously.

'A feeling? You mean a premonition or something?' Anna's face shone in wonder at the idea. That would be something to tell Rob. 'Not scientific,' he would say. But it had worked! It would be something to tell the kids on the school bus next term, too.

Sioned fell silent. She didn't want Anna, in her eagerness for a fantastic story, to broadcast it. It was a secret. A secret between herself and Dinah, though at this moment she had no intention whatsoever of sharing it even with Dinah. It was her own secret. For the time being anyway.

Something began to nag at her thoughts. How *did* it get buried under so much mud? *Why* the strange feelings? She had been so sure that she'd lost it whilst climbing rocks, yet it had called to her, called her away from the mountain, called to her from the depths of the mud.

It could have fallen from her pocket anywhere along the road. Someone like Doubting Thomas could have picked it up and dropped it again. He had visited The Drowned House. 'The House be up,' he had said. If he hadn't said that, they might not have decided to go to The Drowned House at all. It was too puzzling.

They rode on in silence, back along the long stone bridge, beside the lowest lake, and down the road which dipped and rose like a switchback towards Nantyglyn. The more Sioned pondered, trying to explain to herself, the less satisfying were the solutions, but it seemed necessary now to find an explanation. She recalled the dreams. If it hadn't been for the dreams she wouldn't have recognized the triangular room. She shook her head vigorously till her hair swirled round her face, in an effort to clear her mind of the ideas which were constantly posing fresh problems. She wanted no more problems now. She had found what she had been looking for and just wanted to gloat in the magic of it all, and in the relief of knowing that after all, Dinah would soon be able to have the precious cube back in her own safekeeping. Eva would have no cause to throw china at her. The cube would be complete.

They flung their bikes down on the meadow, too weary now to bump them over the grass to the farmyard. Hot and exhausted they flapped their feet through the stone porchway and into the cool dark living-room and dropped into armchairs. Mrs Lind put her head out of the kitchen.

'Oh, *you've* come back, have you? Where've you been?

It must have been important to have missed your dinner so completely.'

'It was,' Anna began dramatically, but Sioned gave her a quick glare. She didn't want her story told. Anna seemed to understand, and carried on, 'I'm ravenous, absolutely starving. We both are. Sorry about missing dinner. Can we get ourselves some Marmite sandwiches or something?'

'You stay where you are,' said Mrs Lind. 'I'll find you something better to eat than that.'

Sounds of bread being cut and buttered came from the kitchen accompanied by the smell of cucumber and tomatoes. Sioned stirred. She was so tired that she felt like a part of the chair.

'I really think I should phone home to say where I am. They might be worrying.'

The telephone was on a wide window seat at the back of the living-room, overlooking what was once a cowshed. Sioned removed a pair of football socks from the receiver and sat beside it to dial, while Anna joined her mother in the kitchen, and almost before she had finished speaking, Mrs Lind had returned with two plates of cheese salad and buttered crusty rolls. They sat in the inglenook and ate ravenously.

'Have you tried putting the piece back yet?' asked Anna through a mouthful of crisp lettuce.

'Not yet. I'll need a table to put it on in case any more pieces drop out.'

'We'll go in that room,' Anna pointed with her knife to a blue door. 'After we've eaten. There's a table in there. And we'll have some peace.'

Robert walked through and Anna groaned.

'We were just hoping to have some peace!' she said.

Robert ignored her. 'Did you find it then?' The sarcastic tone of his voice anticipated a negative answer, but Sioned and Anna both said most positively,

'Yes. We did.'

Robert stopped in his tracks and stared.

'You never did! Don't believe you.'

'Show him, Sioned.'

Sioned opened her hand. There it lay on her sweating palm, embossed like a fossil.

'That's it?' he said in wonder. 'You found that on a mountain?'

'Aha!' Anna tantalized him. 'That's where you're wrong.'

'Bet it was in your pocket all the time.'

'No,' said Sioned firmly. 'I lost it, and found it again.'

'Tell him where, Sioned.'

Sioned gulped, wondering how much to say and where to begin.

'I found it in The Drowned House,' she said simply.

Robert's face was one large question mark.

'There's a house,' said Anna stacking the plates and cutlery ready to take into the kitchen, 'in a valley under a lake. Submerged. But the water level is so low after the drought that the walls are showing. And that's where the ivory was.' She carried the plates smugly away, waiting for Robert to show surprise and envy for their adventure.

'There were crowds of people there,' Sioned added hastily. 'I expect someone picked it up after I had lost it, and dropped it again.'

'Whatever made you think of looking in a place like that?'

Sioned and Anna eyed each other. Anna had been looking forward to this moment when she could tell everyone about Sioned's strange premonition. But it was Sioned's story, not hers. And Sioned wasn't telling.

'Let's go into that room and see if we can put the piece back into the puzzle.'

Sioned unfastened the small bundle from her pocket and tore off the sticky tape. They stepped into the blue-doored room and she set the puzzle down on the table beside the anvil.

'You see,' she said with relish. 'There's the hole, and there's the shape to fit into it.'

'Let me do it!' said Robert and Anna together, lunging forward with such force that they almost overturned the table and sent the precious puzzle sliding gently down the slope. Sioned put out her hand to stop it, and tilted back the table.

'You clumsy thing!' shouted Anna to her brother. 'Let Sioned do it.'

They both agreed to that, and watched as she tried to fit the piece back into the cube, their fingers itching to help her.

Sioned tried to slot the piece in, but it wedged into the wrong position. She took it out, turned it, and tried again. It didn't slip in neatly that way either. She slid, turned, and twisted it.

'I thought it would slip in more easily than this. I'm *sure* it's the right piece,' she said, beginning to feel uncertain whether it was or not. 'It must be.'

'Perhaps it's warped!'

'It must have been loose when it fell out. It couldn't have warped overnight, surely. Ivory doesn't warp, does it?'

'Come on,' said Robert. 'I'll do it for you in a jiffy.' He snatched up the puzzle a split second before Anna's hand reached for it.

'You meany! I wanted to have a go first.' Anna pursed her lips and watched, fidgeting her fingers, hoping he'd fail. He did.

'All right,' he challenged Anna. 'You try, cleversticks.'

'I'll do it,' said Anna hopefully. 'Wait a minute.'

They waited many minutes until Anna, too, had to admit defeat.

'It's absolutely impossible,' she declared. 'I don't believe it was ever in there.'

'It was! Oh, it was!' Sioned wrung her hands. After all the trouble she'd taken to find it! 'It *must* fit. Can't you see? If you look into it it's exactly the right shape.'

'There's only one thing to do,' said Robert wisely. 'We'll have to take it apart and then see if we can fit it in.'

'Oh, no,' said Sioned. 'Supposing they're all as difficult to replace as this one.'

'It's the only thing we can do.'

Sioned supposed it was, so it was decided. The door opened and Mrs Lind brought in some coffee.

'Don't know what you're doing so mysteriously, but I thought maybe you'd like a drink.'

'Thanks, Mum.'

Mrs Lind looked curiously at the puzzle.

'That's nice. What is it?'

'A puzzle,' explained Sioned. 'We're trying to fit a missing piece back.'

'Good luck to you,' Mrs Lind grunted. 'I'm just going to the town shopping. Won't be long.'

There was a scratching sound at the window-pane.

'Anna! Anna, what are you doing?' Nibble's nose was pressed so hard against the glass that it had completely lost its colour.

'Go away!'

They heard the car start up in the yard and Anna went to the window.

'Thank goodness for that,' she said with relief. 'She's taken the little horrors with her.'

They settled themselves on seats around the table and contemplated the task ahead.

'How many pieces did you say?'

'Three hundred and forty three. Seven cubed.'

'Phew! Think of carving that!'

'Think of putting it back together again,' said Sioned with feeling. 'Where do we start?'

'Don't be so gloomy about it,' said Anna kindly. 'We'll do it.'

'I'll get some paper,' suggested Robert.

'Whatever for?'

Robert gave his sister a supercilious glance.

'Because, you ninny, there are *three hundred and forty three* pieces. Can you imagine that lot spread out over the table? We'll have to keep a careful record of each piece we take out so that we know in which order to put them back.'

Sioned had begun to shake the puzzle gently, and to pick at the edges of the shapes in an effort to undo it. She stopped when Robert said that. She could see the wisdom of his words as she remembered the Japanese pig puzzle which had taken her five hours to put back together. And that had only about a dozen pieces.

They could hear Robert coming back across the stone floor of the living-room. Anna bounded out of her chair and slammed the blue door against him.

'We don't want intruders, thank you,' she said distantly. 'It's our puzzle.'

But the door didn't complete its slam, for Robert's toe was just over the threshold. He wriggled it and prised the door open a little wider, throwing his weight against the door.

'Come on, Sioned,' hissed Anna. 'Quickly! Come and lean on the door with me.'

There was a crack and a splinter of wood. The heaving weights on both sides of the door relaxed suddenly, leaving the door swinging precariously on a loose top hinge.

'You did that!' accused Anna sourly.

'You should've let me in.'

'We'll have to do something about it quick, before any-one comes.'

Robert surveyed the damage.

'I'll repair it if you let me help you with the puzzle,' he promised. He found a screwdriver and twisted in the heavy hinge-screws.

'Right,' he said when he was satisfied that all trace of violence had been removed from the door. 'We'll lay out the pieces in order, and I'll make a grid and mark its position. Sioned, you're good at drawing, so you can draw every piece as it comes out, and number it according to its position in my grid.'

'It's not a military manoeuvre,' objected Anna. 'What am I doing?'

'You can get the pieces out.'

'Oh!' Anna was pleased to have been given that task and forgave Robert for being so organizing. She sat down and shook the puzzle.

'Obviously the first one out will be the last one in. And that, of course, is the anvil.' Robert turned the cube over to plot its position. 'We'll call this side ONE, and the position on the grid will be 4E. Understood?'

'Oh, dear!' said Sioned. 'It looks very complicated.'

'It's not at all,' said Robert. He carefully ruled out a net of the cube on paper. Sioned thought it looked like a series of empty crossword puzzles, but she didn't say so.

'Perhaps I'll understand what we're doing as I go along.'

Robert carefully numbered each square, as Sioned shaded the hollows and grooves in her drawing of the anvil.

'Do we call that piece Number One, and label it 4E?'

'You've got the idea,' Robert beamed as he picked up the anvil and placed it at the end of the table, the first in a convoy of three hundred and forty three. 'Don't touch!'

The words jarred in Sioned's ears. Eva had shrieked 'Don't touch!' What would she say if she could see them now?

Anna shook and clawed at the puzzle.

'I think the next one's coming out,' she said excitedly plucking an edge with her nails. 'Yes, here it is!'

A small piece of ivory slid smoothly out and she placed it on the table for Sioned to draw. It was tall and tapered, like an obelisk. Anna rubbed her hands together excitedly.

'Hurry up and draw it, I want to find the next piece.'

'Do you think they represent anything?' said Sioned, drawing the obelisk. 'They look a bit like Chinese lettering.'

'I should think the person who carved that had enough to worry about without making the pieces represent things.'

'Nevertheless, I think I'll give them names. Anvil, obelisk, what's next?'

The third piece was easier to find, and reminded Sioned of a bird. The fourth piece was more difficult, but it was found, and pulled gently out to stand in line behind the anvil, obelisk and bird. Sioned lovingly drew its shape, gave it a name and numbered it twice, once according to its position and once for the order of its removal. Robert methodically marked its place on his network of squares.

'D'you think it was carved out of a solid piece?'

'Yes,' said Robert. 'I think it probably was.' He put down his pencil and mysteriously made for the door. 'And no shutting me out this time!'

He returned holding an open encyclopaedia.

'Look,' he pointed, putting the book on the table. 'Chinese ivory carving. Concentric balls. You must admit they must have been carved from a solid piece.'

'And it looks even more impossible than my cube,' agreed Sioned. 'But aren't they beautiful? Makes me wish I'd carved them. Does it mention anything about cubes, or puzzles?'

They pored over the article on ivory carvings, and scrutinized the photographs, but there was nothing to be compared with the cube.

'It must be unique,' pronounced Sioned proudly, adding in a different tone. 'Wouldn't it have been *awful* if I hadn't found the anvil?'

They carried on dismantling the cube as the hours struck away the time, the cows on the neighbouring farm passed by for milking and Mrs Lind returned from her shopping.

Anna groaned loudly.

'Here comes noise,' she grumbled as the little boys burst out of the car with aeroplane screeches and dived straight for the window.

'Hi! What are you doing in there all the time?'

Anna rose and drew the curtains to shut out the prying eyes.

They continued lining up the ivory pieces until at last they had removed the hundredth piece.

'Let's celebrate,' said Anna with glee. 'I'll bring in some tea.'

They munched biscuits and sipped tea, marvelling at the beauty of each tiny piece standing like soldiers on the mahogany table in front of them. Each surface of each piece was ornately decorated with lines and curves as delicate as strands of cotton.

'It is in good condition,' said Robert. 'How old did Dinah say it was?'

'She didn't. She said nothing about it at all. Just "a problem for you to solve".' Sioned imitated Dinah's croaking voice. 'I say! The ivory anvil is a bit discoloured, I hope she doesn't notice! I'd hate her to think I'd been careless enough to lose it.'

'Never,' said Robert reassuringly. 'How old is she? Ninety-nine? Her eyesight will be failing.'

'Failing?' Sioned spluttered into her tea. 'You should

see her eyes. They're more piercing than anyone's I know. She can see straight into your mind, I'm certain of it. Her eyes are just like black grapes,' she added, recalling the painting of the oriental uncle.

The puzzle was looking less and less like a cube, for the six faces were now barely discernible. All the flat outside edges had been removed and, like a jigsaw without its sides, it left no regular shape. They lined the pieces neatly in rows of forty-nine, and halfway through the third row they decided to leave it until tomorrow, on the table, just as it was.

'Hope we don't get burglars!'

'The little boy's fingers would be far more devastating, and far more likely.'

'We'll have to lock the door.'

All the keys of the house were hung on a hook in the kitchen, on wire loops. They sorted through them and found one which fitted.

'Will they be all right in there?' asked Sioned anxiously. 'I mean, will anyone want to go in there, to use the table?'

'I'll tell Mum they're important and that no one must disturb.'

By this time the little boys were well on their way to bed. As they locked the door Mrs Lind came downstairs folding some clothes. The raucous voices of Nibble and John could be heard singing loudly in the bath.

'Come here, Mum,' hissed Anna. 'Secret!' She unlocked the door again and opened it narrowly. 'Can we leave those there until morning? It's ever so precious and the little ones mustn't touch.'

Mrs Lind laughed.

'Very well,' she promised lightly. 'We won't touch.'

'It's really very important,' begged Anna earnestly. 'They must stay just as they are.'

Mrs Lind looked more serious and a little puzzled.

'Yes,' she said. 'I promise. I'll see no one goes in there.'

'Thanks, Mum.'

Anna turned the key in the lock.

'I'll sleep with it under my pillow,' she whispered to Sioned.

Chapter 7

SIONED should have slept peacefully that night, her hitherto troubled conscience appeased, but in fact she tossed and turned until the bedclothes cork-screwed round her and her pillow felt like cardboard. Eva threw Ming Dynasty vases across the dark room of her half awake mind and they kept shattering, away in the distance. Her mind warped the day's happenings into unorthodox but dramatic episodes so that one minute she found herself in terror and despair in a dank dungeon as a result of her gross carelessness, and the next in a Chinese ancestral home on account of her supreme cleverness. Her head was weary but her restless imagination wove threads of mystery as busily as a spider, and without a pause tied unexpected ends together to produce a tangle of irrelevant and startling solutions.

Early next morning she was awoken by the unusual patter of rain on the window, and saw that the sky outside was dark and heavy. What a blessing it was dry when I was searching for the anvil, she thought thankfully. I wonder how long it will have to rain before the House is drowned again. She felt glad that she had had the rare opportunity of taking Anna to the lakes when the water was so low, and of showing her the House, even if she had, initially, been disappointed by it. In winter she would take her up there again, when the winds howled like angry witches, and when the lakes were brimming and water gushed into them from every groove in the hillside, filling the valley and funnelling with a roar over the dam wall, whipping spray into the air for half a mile or more.

She eyed the *Powys Gazette* as she crunched a piece of blackened toast, and picked it up sharply when her eyes fell on the headline 'Drowned House to be drowned for all time.'

'They've been given the go-ahead for the new dam, Mum. Told you they would. It says here The Drowned House will never again be exposed. The new dam will keep all the lower dams full, it says.'

'Pity,' said her mother cutting some more bread for toasting.

'You should go up there now, Mum, if you can. We went yesterday. It's never been so low. You'll never have another chance, ever, once it rains.'

'P'raps I will.'

Sioned set out as early as she dared for the farm. Anna and Robert were waiting for her eagerly, each one forbidding the other to start without her. The little boys had gathered that something fishy was going on in the front room and were dancing expectantly in the yard when Sioned approached.

'You are not going in that room,' Anna was telling them sternly, wagging the key at them.

'Please. Just a peep?'

'Sioned will let us in, won't you, Sioned? I'll show you some green fungus!'

'Sioned doesn't want to see any green fungus. You can look through the window for one minute if you're good.'

So the little boys gaped through the window, making it misty and sticky, as the older ones continued with the puzzle.

'Two hundred and two, two hundred and three, wait a minute, Anna, you're not giving me time to mark them down.'

The pieces were coming out more willingly now. Anna had discovered that there was a pattern to their order of coming out, and could predict exactly where the next loose piece would be.

'Hurry up, slowcoach,' said Robert, realizing that this time he was waiting for Anna. 'What's the hold-up?'

'Just a moment!' exclaimed Anna, alternately shaking the puzzle and listening. 'I think there's something inside!'

They each held the puzzle to an ear, and shook. Each of them heard an unmistakable rattling sound.

'Let's get on with it,' said Robert. 'We'll soon find it, whatever it is. Next piece, please.'

So many pieces had been removed that some of the cavities now reached through almost to the middle. Anna blew into it.

'Paper!' she announced excitedly. 'I think there's a piece of paper in it.'

'Can't be.'

'Perhaps the person who carved it put it in to stop it rattling?'

'The person who carved this,' said Robert emphatically, 'wouldn't have made a rattly puzzle in the first place.'

'All right. All right,' retorted Anna. 'What do you suggest it is, clever?'

Robert did not offer an answer.

'Next piece, please.'

'Next piece coming up.'

Anna pulled out the next piece, and the next, and the next, and waited for them to be recorded, anxious to uncover whatever was inside it.

'I can see it now,' she exclaimed, trying to tweak it out.

Sioned's page was almost entirely covered now with tiny drawings, and the pieces were lined up in five complete rows on the table. Only two more rows to go. She was enjoying drawing them, feeling in a strange way close to the person who had designed it. Was he a mathematician? A scientist? An artist? Or all three? Whoever it was, he had certainly carved it to perfection and understood the qualities of ivory as a fish understands water. She ran her eyes down the rows of sculptured shapes on her paper.

'No two are alike yet,' she observed. 'He must have been ever so skilled.'

They worked on. Suddenly Anna, daring only to whisper, said,

'I've got it!'

From inside the ivory she carefully drew out a folded piece of paper. She opened it out.

'Writing!' she gasped.

The others dropped their pencils hastily and looked over her shoulder. Anna laid the crinkled paper on the table and stroked out the folds carefully so as not to pull it apart at the creases. In scrawly, curly writing, it said,

'Lizzie Meredith. 1892.'

They stared at each other blankly.

'Then Eva couldn't have done the puzzle,' Sioned murmured. Did this mean that no one had done the puzzle since 1892? And was the last person to do it Lizzie Meredith?

'She must be someone belonging to Dinah and Eva. Their name is Meredith. I wonder how old she would have been when she did the puzzle?'

'Perhaps she was an aunt, or an older sister?'

But Sioned wasn't listening. A picture had flashed into her mind the instant Anna had revealed the writing on the paper. A picture of a little girl with eyes like black grapes, and a frilly pinny, and black boots with buttons on. And somewhere beyond her, the sneering laughter she had heard in her dream. Lizzie Meredith. Was she the girl in her dream?

'Wake up!' Robert's voice startled her from her daydream. 'We're back to work.'

They carried on, conscientiously drawing, marking, and

numbering until at last there were seven complete rows of forty nine spread neatly over the table.

'Don't they look terrific?' Anna said. 'Just think of carving all those. Dad would be ever so interested. Shall we fetch him to see?'

Mr Lind was himself welding a delicate piece of his own sculpture and was slightly annoyed at the interruption.

'You've *got* to come and see, Dad. You *must*. It's the chance of a lifetime.'

He removed his goggles and wiped his forehead with the back of his hand.

'It had better be worthwhile,' he threatened.

When he saw the ivory he agreed that it was. Mrs Lind and the little ones came in to peep, too.

'They all fit together in the shape of a cube,' Anna explained excitedly. 'Look, those are Sioned's drawings of each piece, and Robert's been recording it all scientifically. I've been taking it apart. Now we're going to try and put it all back together again.'

'The best of luck,' breathed Mr Lind. 'It's likely to take years.'

'Not years!' said Sioned. 'Dinah might die!' A few days ago she had wished that poor old Dinah would die, but now she reversed her wish. Old Dinah *mustn't* die before she returned the puzzle. That would be terrible!

The little boys were less curious now that they had been allowed to peep, so that they were able to continue without intermittent tapping at the window and shouts of 'Hello!' Anna locked the door and they settled quietly to replace all the pieces.

'We mustn't forget to put Lizzie Meredith's piece of paper back,' said Sioned.

'No,' pleaded Anna. 'Let's keep it as evidence! Otherwise no one will believe.'

'I think we should put it back,' said Sioned. 'It belongs to the puzzle now.'

As it was Sioned's puzzle they both agreed, and folded up the paper into its original small square.

'But I know what we could do!' she added, suddenly standing as though the idea had hit with a force from underneath. 'Let's write our own names on a piece of paper, and put it in with Lizzie's.'

They all found it an appealing idea.

'Do you think another piece of paper would fit in?'

'It would have to be very fine.'

'I know just the thing,' said Robert dashing out of the room. He returned with a piece of fine, translucent paper.

'Architect's tracing paper,' he said.

'That's just right,' approved Sioned, feeling its quality. The occasion demanded, above all, quality.

In silence they signed their names in tiny writing with waterproof Indian ink and a mapping pen, and Sioned added the date with the dignity of one who signs a wedding certificate or a peace treaty. They cut it as small as they could round the writing, and folded it.

'We'll have to make up part of the puzzle first, and then push the paper inside. We can't hope to make the puzzle round two bits of paper.'

They took one last look at the writing of Lizzie Meredith and settled to remake the cube. The clock struck eleven.

'Let's time ourselves. See how long it takes.'

It took them most of the day, and by tea-time they were stuck. Completely and utterly stuck. They had fixed the first few pieces together by sharing fingers, holding and balancing until the pieces clung together of their own accord. Each piece slipped neatly into its snug cavity and each square was methodically filled in on the grid to denote that it was home. But the three hundredth piece refused.

'We were doing *so* well,' sighed Sioned loudly. 'I thought it was too good to be true. Now we're in a worse position than before we started.' She let her despairing chin drop to her knuckles. 'Only forty-three to go and we're stuck,' she said bitterly.

'Lizzie Meredith must have done it,' said Robert, picking up the puzzle yet again. 'Surely we can!'

'She must have been a genius.'

He pushed and twisted, and coiled and shook, but it was of no use. They were at a standstill. Sioned's heart sank to her toes.

Mrs Lind tapped on the door and opened it.

'It's getting late. Would Sioned like to stay for tea?'

Sioned didn't know what to say. She didn't want to leave the puzzle again.

'I suppose I might as well go home,' she said miserably. 'We're stuck.'

'Oh dear,' sympathized Mrs Lind. 'Have you fitted back the missing piece yet?'

'No. It was the first one out so it must be the last . . .'

Sioned's words faded into silence and all three of them looked hopefully to the ivory anvil standing at the tail of the procession, slightly discoloured from its adventure.

'That's it!' shouted Robert. He reached over and grabbed it eagerly, and within a few seconds it had slotted into position.

'But if it belongs there, how did it come to drop out first?'

No one knew the answer to that, but it didn't matter, for it fitted like a hand in a glove, as did the next piece, and the next.

'I'd like to stay, if it's not too much bother,' said Sioned, hoping that Mrs Lind wouldn't object to her changing her mind.

'Yes, dear. Of course you may. Don't forget to phone home and tell them you're here.' She closed the door softly behind her.

It was early evening and the bats were out when the last piece, the obelisk, was pushed into its hole.

'Of course that would have been first out. It's the only one that could possibly slide out by itself.'

'Lizzie Meredith must have made a mistake and put it back in the wrong order.'

'But it must be far more difficult to rebuild the wrong way than the right!'

'It doesn't matter how, or when, or where,' sang Sioned thrusting her stiff but delighted fingers up in the air. 'It's done, done, done!'

She rolled up her page of drawings, and put the completed puzzle safely into its polythene bag, confidently longing for the moment when at last she could present it to Dinah.

'I'll take it to her first thing in the morning.'

But deep sleep carried her right past first thing in the morning, and when eventually she did present herself downstairs, her father had a morningful of jobs lined up for her.

'Oh, Dad, do I have to?' she pleaded.

'Go on, girl! it won't take long,' he chivvied her cheerfully. 'There'll be plenty of morning left when this is done.'

She fetched her bike out and filled her saddlebag carefully. First there was a batch of letters to post, and some to deliver personally, followed by two bottles of medicine to take to isolated farms where the people were too ill or aged to collect it themselves.

She arrived at the first deserted farm and looked round the yard for someone to whom she could give the packet. The house was in darkness and there was no sound except from the cows, curiously watching her from the gate. She had just decided to leave it in the porch when a small lady sprouted in front of her, wrapped in a huge blanket snugly as a mushroom in its skin.

'Thank you de-ah,' she said, separating each syllable with the precision of a metronome. 'Come in and have a Welsh-cake.'

'No. No, thank you. It's very kind, but . . .'

But – she was shuffled in through the low cottage doorway and placed firmly on a tall-backed settle, and, biting a rather tough Welshcake, had to listen to the old lady's history, some recent, some ancient, flowing concurrently like tangled strings of beads.

She fidgeted and tried to listen. The narrow wooden seat made furrows in the underside of her thighs and a ridge dug sharp teeth into her backbone, so that she began to ponder over the question of why a settle was called a settle, since that was the last thing a person could do in one.

The second bottle of medicine was easier. It only involved an old man's old-fashioned, stick-poking jokes and teasing which required no more than a smile and a giggle at the right moments, and she was away.

Dinah kicked a wedge under the door which divided her territory from Eva's, and walked with agitated steps back into the shop. She picked up a duster and dabbed half-heartedly at the darkened rims of beflowered chamber-pots which lived on the shelves behind the counter. She wanted to stand by the shop door, to see if *she* was coming, but she carried on with her dusting instead, as doubts flowed over her whether she had been right about the ivory, and the girl. She felt tired. Her hopes were as weak as a crazed saucer, and Eva, on the other side of the door, was seething and bubbling beneath the surface. Any moment now she would let fly. Oh, where was Sioned Jones with the ivory?

Dinah felt frail and almost defeated. She might even have to admit that Eva had been right. She shouldn't have given it away.

She put down her duster and went into the back room. Eva could be heard muttering and mumbling like a trapped bluebottle behind the wedged door. Dinah sat down in her rocking chair and closed her eyes in a fruitless effort to shut out the bluebottle noises. She rocked faster, making the chair creak, and her face relaxed. The creaking drowned the sounds she didn't want to hear. She was tired of Eva. Tired of china. Tired of waiting. The chair sank to stillness and slumber came and shaded her from the world like a black umbrella.

Chapter 8

SIONED's heart was singing as she hurried down the street towards Dinah's dark shop. She would be able to look Dinah straight in the eye and say proudly, 'I've done the puzzle.' She wouldn't twitch, or giggle, or divulge an inkling about the loss of the anvil. The puzzle was all back in one piece again and her conscience was as clear as the bright crystal morning. She looked up at the sparkling sky with wisps of white cloud floating like her own carefree soul, and began to skip joyfully.

'Watch out, girl!' a sharp voice scolded as she nearly collided with the foot of a ladder. Winnie the Wash was cleaning her windows.

'Sorry.'

She skipped beneath the ladder defying bad luck to befall her and clutched the puzzle. Dinah would be so pleased that she had done it. 'A little problem for you to solve,' she had said. Well, Dinah China, the problem's solved, and it's coming back to you. Her skipping feet slapped out a rhythm on the paving stones and she turned the words into a song in her head. It's coming back to you. It's coming back to you. Hasn't been done for eighty years and it's coming – back – to you.

She stopped skipping. Could the girl in her dream have been Lizzie Meredith? If she was, however could she find out for certain? No one else could see into her mind to examine the memory of an old dream. She couldn't even describe her very vividly. A girl about her own size, with dark hair rather like her own, an abundance of frilly Victorian clothes, and a strange air of familiarity in the way she moved. The description would be too vague. The dream girl was more like a feeling than a person. She couldn't even have formed an Identikit picture from such a flimsy memory. 'Have you seen this face?' No, she would never be able to find out for certain who the dream girl was.

But she could find out more about Lizzie, if she dared. 'Who was Lizzie Meredith?' She only had to say those four simple words. Old Dinah would know who Lizzie was. She would perhaps remember her in frilly clothes with black buttoned boots and long dark hair, rather thin, quiet, maybe a little sad. The picture would match her dream in every detail, and at last she would know.

She started skipping and began to embroider a life round Lizzie. She would have been a sweet child, a little older than Eva. How difficult it was to imagine someone older than Eva! The little Meredith sisters would have been very fond of her of course, and would have played spinning tops and marbles with her, and made daisy chains. Perhaps they had watched her bury her name inside the ivory puzzle. Sioned quickly unpicked the stiches of that idea. That would be a secret between herself and Lizzie.

'Shall I ask? Or shall I not?' she pondered as her feet, momentarily clad in Lizzie's dainty black boots counted the paving stones. Shall I ask? Shall I not? Shall I? Shall I not? The last paving stone told her most decidedly not, but she ignored its advice. I'll ask about Lizzie and I shall tell Dinah all about the name inside the puzzle, she declared boldly to herself. I'll get the whole matter cleared up.

The brown door opened with its usual clang and she stepped down on to the squeaky dry floorboards and inhaled the dust of ancient china. Lifeless faces of porcelain shepherdesses and Toby jugs stared blindly, and a spider spun a new web in a distant corner. Outside, a lorry crunched along the gritty road and bike pedals clicked, but they were noises from another world. Dinah's shop held a silence in its hands which was stronger than all sound. Sioned breathed shallowly so as not to stir the solid silence, and waited, but no Dinah came.

She could hear her own heart patter, bursting with eagerness to pull out the puzzle and lay it before Dinah's eyes on the counter. But there were no sounds to indicate the approach of Dinah.

Where are you, Dinah? Why don't you come?

I hope she's not dead! Sioned paled at the thought. Don't be dead, Dinah, please don't be dead. Not now.

Her eyes wandered to the door at the back of the shop. Perhaps at this very moment Dinah was dying of despair from having had to wait so long for the puzzle. Fear poked its cold fingers at her. Should she creep to the door to see if old Dinah was all right? But what would she find? How could she distinguish between life and death in someone so very old, and whichever it was, what could she do about it?

She waited a little longer, and then went outside and came in again, giving the brown door an extra sharp jerk. The clapper of the bell hammered back and forth furiously, showing no sign of stopping. Shh! she said to it. Not so loud. I don't want to appear too impatient even if I am.

At last the door at the back of the shop moved. It must be Dinah. It must be Dinah.

It was Dinah. There she stood like a genie summoned by the magic lamp. All Sioned's fears took flight and she smiled widely with relief.

'I've done it,' she said eagerly, nodding her head to confirm her words. 'I've done your puzzle, solved the problem.'

She took it out of her pocket and set it down on the counter. The soft paper fell apart revealing the small white cube, complete.

'I took it to pieces and did it again,' she explained once more.

Why wasn't Dinah saying anything? Why was she looking so oddly at the puzzle? She was picking it up, turning it over. Sioned's spirits fell and she backed towards the door. She knows! Somehow old Dinah knows! Sioned gazed, horror-stricken, and unable to escape, as Dinah, with one black eye fixed firmly on her, examined all the surfaces of the cube. Any moment now she would notice that the anvil was discoloured. She'd be angry. She might even throw china!

Her hand fumbled for the door handle in the darkness behind her as she watched Dinah's face, forecasting a terrible storm.

But Dinah wasn't angry. Dinah had begun to smile, to beam. Her grey old face lit up in a way Sioned had never seen before, and she began to mumble, in her low, slow voice. Sioned leaned forward, straining her ears. *What* was the old woman saying?

'... lost it ... Ty-Rhonwen ...' Sioned swallowed hard '... the valley ... Lizzie ...'

She knew everything! Her black grapelike eyes had guessed all, had seen that Sioned had tried to deceive her.

'Good-bye, Miss Meredith,' she said as firmly as her trembling voice would allow. She backed to the door again, away from this terrifying old lady. Words still rasped from Dinah's mouth and floated disjointedly across the darkness to Sioned.

A load of rubbish, Sioned tried to convince herself. Dinah's moithering, doesn't know what she's saying. She can't possibly know that I lost a piece.

She opened the door and catapulted out on to the pavement like a wild bird out of a cage.

But Dinah's words came with her. Lost it. Lost it. Ty-Rhonwen.

Sioned felt too stunned to move. The sky had darkened and large drops of rain made black patches on the paving stones. She watched them multiply as she turned Dinah's words over in her mind. Ty-Rhonwen. That was the name of The Drowned House. How had she known about that? Had she really been watching? It was uncanny. She had gabbled about uncles and aunts and cousins, and all her mutterings were interspersed with 'lost it'. And – had she mentioned the name 'Lizzie'?

The wind whipped rain into her face and she began to run down the street, away from Dinah, away from china. Winnie the Wash had taken her ladder in and people were putting up their umbrellas. Sioned didn't stop to collect her bike. The shop was full. It would take ages to get through. She ducked beneath umbrellas and dodged clusters of farmers and shoppers, past the ice-cream shop and the greengrocer's and on down the hill to the river. It was raining heavily now, but still she ran on.

How did old Dinah know, she kept asking herself. How? She paused for breath as a new meaning to old Dinah's words crept over her. Supposing Sioned Jones had not lost the ivory anvil? Supposing someone like Lizzie Meredith had lost it, years and years ago?

The idea seemed to fit like an old cap. For Dinah had known about Lizzie, she had mentioned her name, together with that of The Drowned House. And she had murmured that something had been lost. Sioned backed into a doorway as the rain became heavier but it did not shelter her from the shivers of panic that invaded her. If Dinah had known everything, had known it all along, then she must have chosen Sioned to find it for her. To find something buried deep under the mud and drowned beneath many millions of gallons of water for nearly a century. *And she had found it!*

Sioned edged out of the doorway and pressed on towards Anna's farm. She would tell Anna all about it. That would take away the fear and make it all seem funny and unreal, for Anna wouldn't take it seriously at all. She would laugh and joke and burst the bubble of fear for ever.

The rain was heavier than ever now. She would have to stop again. She found a shop doorway and stood in it but it was only one step deep and didn't protect her much. She pushed up her collar but rain trickled down her sodden fringe and ran on to her nose. She blew the cold drips away and shook her head to flick off surplus raindrops.

A shoal of boys on bikes plunged across the road leaving trails of dry ribbons which criss-crossed the shiny wet surface. They cascaded over the bump and filtered left, down into Church Lane. Sioned turned the corner after them. Below her the church gates were firmly shut, and hordes of small boys scrambled excitedly up the wrought ironwork like monkeys. Of course. Today was Miss Hopkin's wedding. They'd be tying the gates. She made her way towards the crowds waiting outside the gates, where fat ladies whispered confidentially beneath dripping umbrellas.

'Eight bridesmaids, all in rainbow colours, they say.'

'There's only seven colours in the rainbow, Ma!'

'Be quiet, boy!'

'Silk top hats.'

'They might throw a lot of money, Ma. Maybe fifty pence pieces.'

'Used to be threepenny bits in my day.'

'Them little silver joeys.'

'Handfuls of them.'

'Half-crowns sometimes, mind, if it was someone posh.'

'Like Miss Hopkin and this bloke.'

'Tommy! Don't say "bloke" at a wedding. It's not nice.'

Sioned found a space in the iron bars and slipped her face between them. If there were to be eight bridesmaids in rainbow colours and men in silk top hats it would be worth waiting to see. The sky brightened again and waterdrops glistened from the creeping ivy on the gravestones. Sioned's eyes wandered up the long driveway to the church door where the bridal procession would soon appear.

Perhaps Lizzie Meredith, too, was married in this church. Perhaps like today, the boys of seventy or eighty years ago had fastened the gates and refused to cut them until a handful of coins was tossed over them into the roadway. Perhaps she was christened here, in the stone font. Christened, married, and buried.

Buried! Sioned's eyes flitted from headstone to headstone. If she had been buried here there would be evidence, on a gravestone. *Here lies Lizzie Meredith.*

'Let me through,' she pleaded with the biggest boy who was checking that the gates were still securely tied. 'Please let me through.'

'Naw – they'll be comin' out soon, mun.'

'Through the side gate. You needn't have tied that. Brides never come out through the side gate, especially Miss Hopkin.'

'No. Too late. They'll be 'ere any minute now.'

Behind the cottages near the river was a piece of waste ground where people threw dead flowers. Sioned squeezed through a gap in the hedge and picked her way over the faded, fermenting flowers. She remembered how she used to make scent out of rose petals in old medicine bottles when she was small. The resulting smell had always been a disappointment to her. She sniffed. This graveyard for flowers smelt just the same as her rose perfume and she held her breath to keep out the stupefying odours. After climbing the high church wall she found herself in a wilderness of forgotten tombstones at the back of the church.

She read the names engraved on the slabs of stone with painstaking care. David Pugh. John Williams and his wife Mary. Another David Pugh who died young. There were Prices, Evanses, Hugheses, Joneses. 1784. 1872. 1801. No Merediths. She wandered in and out of the graves, tripping over neglected edges and scratched by the long grass.

The church bells began to peal and sing-song voices filled the air. Sioned stood up from where she was kneeling and moved across to the yew tree to watch the bride. The sun had once more burst through the greyness making the churchyard steamy like a tropical jungle. Through the mist she saw a photographer like a big game hunter line up his camera ready for the kill. He winked through his camera and shot, adjusted his tripod, and shot again. On either side of Miss Hopkin four small bridesmaids bloomed like fresh flowers. More photographs. Then at last with great ostentation and babbling and more shooting they proceeded towards the church gates. The back of the procession wasn't as pretty as the front so Sioned returned to the wilderness of graves.

In loving memory of . . . Here lieth the body of . . . Rest in Peace. But not a single Meredith anywhere. Where were they all? Did the Merediths live for ever?

She examined a pair of dark grey stones polished on the front surfaces until they shone like marble, scrutinized crumbling yellow stones, read inscriptions on stones with pillars carved in the shapes of angels. Her fingertips traced the stony floral arrangements and the extravagant flourishes of serifs coiling like snakes at corners. She laughed, or wondered, or felt touched by different epitaphs. But nowhere was there an epitaph written in memory of a Meredith.

In the distance she heard a shower of tinkling coins being

tossed over the gates and on to the lane, where small boys skidded in their best shoes to grab what they could.

'Cut the ropes now, boy.'

A knife sawed through the ropes and the huge iron gates creaked open to let the bride and her retinue through. Sioned turned to follow, to see if any fifty pence pieces had been thrown, and to see the boys torment Miss Hopkin further by tying old boots and tin cans to the back of her car. Sioned's foot, as she turned, nipped the edge of a pebble and sent it tiddly-winking across the path. Behind a clump of willow-herb she heard it hit a stone. There must be one there that she had missed. She waded through the long grass and parted it gently with her hands. At last the name Meredith met her eyes. She pushed aside a hogweed plant and read,

HERE LIETH THE BODY OF ANN, WIFE OF
SAMUEL MEREDITH, WHO DEPARTED THIS LIFE
THE FIFTH DAY OF OCTOBER, 1884,
AT THE AGE OF THIRTY-SIX YEARS

Sioned sat back on her heels, disappointed. Not Lizzie. The only Meredith in the churchyard and it had to be an Ann. And a Samuel. But not Lizzie.

She parted the undergrowth further to see if Samuel had been buried beside his wife, and gasped with disbelief as she read,

AND OF LIZZIE, HER DAUGHTER, DIED FIFTEENTH
OF AUGUST, 1894, AT THE AGE OF SIXTEEN YEARS.

So Lizzie, poor Lizzie, had not inherited the family virtue of longevity. She had died at the tender age of sixteen, in 1894, just two years after hiding her name in the puzzle.

Sioned ran her fingers over the name and read on. There was a short epitaph at the bottom of the stone. She cleared earth and stones and thick weed away from the small lettering etched in the crumbling and darkened stone. It was barely discernible, and it was in Welsh, she realized as her fingers felt the abundance of Ys and Ws. Welsh poetry would not be at all easy to translate. But she picked out a line of words which immediately touched her heart without any necessity for translation.

Y mae Ty-Rhonwen yn drist, she read softly. 'Rowena's House is sad.' She supposed it must be, losing Lizzie and her mother, and then being pulled down to make way for water. The Drowned House. So that was why Dinah had muttered its name. Lizzie Meredith and her mother had lived and died there. But what about Samuel, her father? There was no mention of his death. She read the carved name again. Samuel Meredith. The name hooked a picture from the back of her mind. A picture of black grapes and flowers and a Chinese vase with dragons on it. Dinah's uncle's painting. She screwed up her eyes to recall every detail. The signature at the bottom right hand corner was 'Samuel Meredith'.

She leaned back on a headstone which rested crookedly behind her. So Lizzie's father was Dinah's oriental uncle. She cupped her chin in her hands to do the appropriate arithmetic. Assume that Dinah was born in 1880. Lizzie would only have been two years older. Dinah would certainly have known her, and her father. And if Samuel's wife and child had departed this life so soon, he would have had no family, just Dinah and Eva. Dinah had said that their uncle looked after them as children. The dates fitted neatly.

Sioned felt elated with the satisfaction of finding, for once, a correct solution to an arithmetical problem. Perhaps poor Samuel went to China to escape the triple tragedy of losing first his wife, then his child, and finally his house. That must be why his name wasn't on the stone. He must have died in China.

Sioned skipped down the church path and whistled a tune.

She had the whole history of the Meredith family nicely ironed out. Now she was free to embellish it as much as her imagination required.

I wonder if you know me, Lizzie Meredith, wherever you are. I think you might know a bit about me, Lizzie, for I have your old boot-button in my pocket. And you and I alone know about the secret inside the puzzle. And Anna and Robert, of course, but they don't count. Thank you for helping me to find the ivory anvil, for I'm sure you did, even though I don't believe in ghosts. I'm sorry you died so young. I would have liked you. But if you had lived long enough to meet me you would have been a very old lady. Perhaps it's better as it is.

There was no trace of Miss Hopkin's wedding when Sioned creaked through the high gates, just one or two bedraggled boys searching the ditches to see if the others had missed any silver coins. She headed towards Anna's farm.

Another torrent threatened and she stopped beneath the railway arch to shelter. A dustbin lorry passed close by, muddy water squirting up from each wheel; and dustbin lorries, she thought crossly, have nothing whatsoever to do with Lizzie, or ivory anvils or strange feelings which stir your heart. She felt indignant at the interruption of so mundane a vehicle into the world of Lizzie Meredith.

Lizzie Meredith. A name carved behind a tangle of weeds on a headstone and scrawled across a tiny piece of paper. No more. Lizzie Meredith, who were you?

Anger overcame Sioned. Why hadn't she asked Dinah who Lizzie was, while she had had the opportunity? Dinah would have known. She had muttered her name, and their ages were so close.

She found herself clanging clumsily through Dinah's shop door. A cobweb brushed her cheek as she moved towards the counter where Dinah still stood. She was just about to apologize for her rude exit, but stopped herself.

Dinah was still mumbling and nodding as though Sioned had never left. She peered behind her at the shop door. The bell was still swinging gently. She *had* just come through it. She *had* visited the churchyard and watched the wedding. And Dinah was still standing as though no time had passed at all.

Without daring to anticipate Dinah's reaction she blurted out,

'Who was Lizzie Meredith?'

'What do you know about her?'

Dinah's words pounced on top of hers and the black eyes pierced her own.

'Not – nothing really,' she stammered. But Dinah's eyes demanded more. Sioned felt her voice stumbling over the words she did not want to say.

'I just went into the churchyard. Her name was on a gravestone. I just wondered . . .'

'Come,' barked Dinah. She picked up the puzzle and disappeared into the back room. Sioned followed her through the door and into the darkness. Dimly she saw Dinah place the ivory puzzle amongst the clutter on the mantlepiece and gesture to her to sit down. Sioned wriggled herself up on to a long-legged bentwood chair near Eva who was huddled on a stool in the corner.

'Hello, Miss Meredith,' she said as pleasantly as she possibly could, anxious to keep on the right side of Eva. She didn't want any flying china to cross her path.

'She was asking about Lizzie,' Dinah explained.

'Great gormless girl,' Eva spat out.

Sioned nearly leapt out of her skin in astonishment at such an accusation and sought for words to apologize for her inquisitiveness.

' 'Orrible big bully, she was.'

'Al'ays bossin' us littl'uns about.'

'Sneering, and making fun.'

'A real terror, was Lizzie.'

Sioned gaped incredulously. The relief of discovering that they weren't talking about her was offset by a feeling of annoyance. How dared they disillusion her? Calling poor Lizzie such dreadful names! They were painting a vicious picture which made her own image of Lizzie as unreal as a paper doll. Huge, bullying, ungainly, unmerciful! Oh, they were slandering Lizzie dreadfully! They were making her out to be some monster.

Sioned felt saddened. Her own idea had been so much sweeter. It served her right for asking. So the girl in the dream had no significance at all, just an ordinary, hazy, dream-ghost.

'Blamed us for losing it, she did,' Eva was snorting.

'You did,' accused Dinah.

'I never. You did.'

' 'Twas a' accident. Slipped between floorboards.'

'Your fault.'

'Yours.'

They sulked for a while and sucked in their lips. When they started talking again their old voices ran together like waters in a mountain stream and Sioned had to concentrate very hard to follow the meandering path. As she listened the memories sprouted and flowered in the weed-tangled gardens of their minds, and she picked, and pruned, and re-arranged, and gradually a story emerged which began to make sense.

It was almost impossible to imagine that Eva and Dinah had ever been two mischievous little girls, but it was quite clear that they had been. The little rascals had stolen cousin Lizzie's precious ivory puzzle whilst they were staying at their uncle's home, Ty-Rhonwen, and had sneaked it down to the garden-room to take to pieces. They had an idea that Lizzie had hidden something inside it and they wanted to find out what the secret was. But they never did, because as they were taking it apart a piece fell to the ground and slipped between the floorboards, and Lizzie had burst in on them as they were trying to retrieve it with a toothpick.

'Thumped us 'ard, old Lizzie did.'

'And pulled our 'air. Oh, she was a terror.'

'And then, when she saw that bit 'ad gone – ooh!' Dinah's memories made her shudder, and they both fell into silence once more.

'Was the lost piece shaped a bit like an anvil?' Sioned asked warily.

'Yes, yes,' Dinah muttered impatiently. 'That bit you found.'

Sioned jumped. What *didn't* these two old ladies know?

''Aunts us, she does,' whispered Eva, drawing a grubby shawl over her shoulders, and Dinah nodded her head in agreement.

'Said she'd never let us rest till we found it. And she never has.'

''Aunts us,' repeated Eva with a grimace.

'But – but it's all right now. That bit's been found.'

A glimmer of a smile lit the two old faces as they realized that for the first time in their lives they were free of the nightmare Lizzie. Sioned shared in their smile, happy that at last she had made a comment which had not brought displeasure.

'We can go now,' grunted Dinah contentedly. 'In peace.'

'Where?' puzzled Sioned. Where could someone as old as Dinah possibly want to go?

'Over the wall.' Dinah pointed East and shut her eyes peacefully. 'The cemetery.'

'Oh, no!' Sioned almost shouted. 'You mustn't think of things like that.' She bit her lip and looked at Dinah's wrinkled eyelids. What a stupid thing to say to one so old. She supposed, sadly, that at nearly a hundred Dinah would be thinking of it a great deal.

'Anyway,' said Sioned, intending to cheer her. 'The puzzle is complete now, so Lizzie would have been pleased. And she was very young when she died,' she added, just in case Dinah was dreading the possibility of meeting up with her in some future life.

' 'Twas 'er own fault, that was,' Eva shouted sharply.

Oh, goodness, what have I said now?

'She would go back to look for it.'

'They all told her not to.'

'Stubborn as an ole mule.'

'They'd started on the House. The stones were loose.'

' 'Er own fault. Not ours.'

So that was the reason they had been haunted by the memory of Lizzie's threats? She had gone back to Ty-Rhonwen just as it was being demolished, in the hope of recovering the missing anvil. But she had been hit by falling masonry, and died. And that had been the end of Lizzie.

But it wasn't the end of Lizzie as far as little Eva and Dinah were concerned. In their minds she had grown to monstrous proportions, for they fully believed they had been the cause of her untimely death. Poor Dinah and Eva, having to wait eighty years to be free of her, until the water was low enough to expose the triangular garden room, until someone came along to find it for them.

Someone like me! The enormity of the completed task suddenly overwhelmed Sioned and she became deaf to the words of the two old ladies.

Her eyes settled on Lizzie's puzzle on the mantelpiece. No vibrations. No silent signals. It was at peace now, like Dinah and Eva. In the darkness of this room it became clear to her that it had been the puzzle which had guided her up the valley to Ty-Rhonwen. Drawn towards the anvil as to a magnet, it had pulled her along with it. Eva had been right about its power. Now, after its brief exposure to daylight, it would probably be buried again in the blackness of the trunk, its mission fulfilled, its power at rest.

The two old voices dwindled wearily beside her, the words indistinguishable now, the faces oblivious of her presence. She slid down from her chair and prepared to slip away.

'My dream was right.' Dinah's voice was weak but triumphant.

'Rubbish,' said Eva.

Sioned paused at the door. Dinah had a dream?

The old lady looked up at her.

'I had a dream, Sioned fach, many years ago, Just a lumper I was then. It was just the spot where the ivory slipped through the floor, where she was digging, just the spot.' She closed her eyes and began to rock.

'Nonsense,' snorted Eva. 'Can't believe in dreams.'

'Ah! This one was different. I al'ays knew this one would come true. She was digging in the corner, and found the ivory. I couldn't understand the mud at the time though. Not the mud.' Dinah opened an eye and cast a glance at Sioned.

Sioned felt her flesh prickle as she looked back at the glistening eye. Dinah's prophetic dream had been identical with her own! Now she knew why the girl's mannerisms had been so familiar, now she understood the feeling of shared despair, and the strange sensation that Dinah had been watching over her as she had dug in the mud. The dream girl had been *herself*. It could have been no one else.

She had taken part, like an actor, in Dinah's dream, and

it was the young Dinah herself who had dressed her dream in frilly clothes and black boots. So that in her own dream she had caught a glimpse of herself as seen through Dinah's childish Victorian eyes.

The puzzle glowed softly in the thick darkness and here, in Dinah's back room, it was easy to imagine that a dream could have hung on a cobweb for nearly a century, dislodged only by the ivory's sudden release of power and wafted away one night like fluff on the breeze, to be caught for an instant by her own sleeping mind.

The room was silent now, save for the heavy breathing of the two old ladies as they drifted into a shallow sleep. She could leave now. She had found out everything she wanted to know. All she needed now was to find Anna.

She was bursting to tell someone, to have someone share the wonder of it all. But would Anna believe her? Anna, who had not sensed the magic of the singing on the hill? Anna, who knew so well how to deal with teasing boys and irritating brothers but didn't understand the poetry of a lost language? She no longer wanted Anna to laugh, to disperse her fears. She wanted her to believe, to understand.

She hung undecided under the railway arch and listened to the patter of rain weakening. The sky brightened once more and the wet road glistened.

Sioned shaded her eyes with her hand as she watched a figure silhouetted high on the mountain road above her. It was Anna, dancing wildly and waving her arms.

'What do you think?' she yelled when she was near enough for it to be worthwhile yelling. 'They've been putting new signs on our road. Welsh ones!'

Sioned blinked. *Anna* was excited about Welsh road signs?

She smiled and a huge wave of relief from all sorts of anxieties flowed out with the smile.

'So they haven't forgotten that Nantyglyn is Welsh, after all,' she said happily.

'Perhaps the language is coming back just as you hoped it would,' Anna went on eagerly. 'Perhaps we'll all be speaking Welsh again in Nantyglyn, indeed-to-goodness look-you!'

A week ago, thought Sioned, I'd have felt like hitting you for that. But now she laughed. She would find her old Welsh books and start learning again. *Yr wyf fi, yr wyt ti, y mae ef, mae hi.* And this time she wouldn't stop.

'I'll teach you to speak Welsh,' she told Anna. 'And then I'll have someone to talk to.'

Anna was delighted.

'Then Robert won't be able to understand a word we're saying.'

'What do the signs say?' Sioned asked.

Anna spat out an unpronounceable string of home-made syllables. 'Then underneath, *underneath* mark you, "mountain road" in English.'

Sioned lifted her hands to the stormy sky and whooped with delight.

'They'll be having "Open" and "Closed" on shop doors again and children will play Welsh conkers in the street and I'll be able to read *The Mabinogion.*'

A cloud burst above them as they made their way to the farm, Sioned eagerly expressing her theories about the ivory anvil and Lizzie Meredith, and Anna listening intently. There was something wonderfully refreshing about a downpour of rain.

They turned into the gate of the meadow, true friends now, their souls enmeshed by an unbreakable bond. Sioned put her hand into her pocket. It felt strangely empty now. But she was free, free from the ivory anvil, free from Dinah, free to share secrets with Anna, and free to carve her alabaster.

A new idea was forming in her mind and like a revelation she knew exactly what she was going to carve. Three by three by three instead of seven by seven by seven. Alabaster was softer than ivory, so the pieces would have to be bigger and simpler, but they would fit together as satisfyingly as the ivory had, into a perfect cube. She would carve a puzzle like the Chinese ivory cube, but from alabaster. She'd do it, even if it took a hundred years to work out the mathematics of it.

And she would let Anna into that secret, too.

ABOUT THE AUTHOR

Sylvia Fair was born in Rhayader, Mid-Wales, and went to Llandrindod Wells Grammar School, then trained as an art teacher at the Bath Academy of Art. She is now married, has five children and lives in Lincolnshire.

Two other Puffins

ALISON MORGAN

RUTH CRANE

Ruth's father had died in a road accident, and her mother and sister lay injured in hospital. She was still Ruth Crane, the clever American girl, but now they might be poor, they might even live in Llanwern, the simple Welsh village where her mother had grown up, and Ruth felt that a little knowledge of cooking and cleaning would have been more useful than all her brains and book-learning. She also had her young brother Tony to cope with, and now they were on their own together at their aunt's house, Ruth was beginning to see some sense in him at last. People were interesting, she thought, and cookery too, and she was going to learn plenty about both.

JEAN CRAIGHEAD GEORGE

JULIE OF THE WOLVES

Miyax lay on her stomach, watching the wolves. She was trembling with hunger and fear, not of the wolves but because it was seven days since she had run away from home. She would find her way to the coast, she thought, and there she would take a ship south to San Francisco, and find her American pen-friend in the white house on the hill. There she would use her American name, Julie, and learn to curl her hair, and forget the old Eskimo ways that had trapped her into marrying her strange, frightening husband.

Jean George likes and understands animals *and* people, and as a result this enthralling but simply told story won the coveted Newbery Medal for the best American book of fiction for children in 1973.